PRAISE FOR *THE DH*

T0115828

"With humor, strong examples, and timeless wisdom, Bortolin offers a new way to think about a pop culture phenomenon. Lead us to Yoda, he does."—*Publishers Weekly*

"A good introduction to the teachings of Buddha and how they infuse the characters of Star Wars—on both the light and dark sides of the force."—*SFRevu*

"A welcome and enlightening addition to Star Wars, opening up a new way to understand the narrative of this beloved series." —Sumi Loundon, editor of *Blue Jean Buddha*

"A wise and accessible book."—Jana Riess, author of *What Would Buffy Do?*

"This entertaining and insightful primer provides a useful service to film buffs who want to better understand the real-life religion behind this popular fictional world. Bortolin succeeds in ferreting out some real wisdom from the films, providing a Buddhist interpretation of the Jedi Way."—*Tricycle*

"Fans of either Yoda or the Buddha will find *The Dharma of Star Wars* an enjoyable, informative read." —Keith Kachtick, author of *Hungry Ghost*

"The Star Wars saga takes place in a galaxy far, far away, but *The Dharma of Star Wars* demonstrates quite effectively that the universal truths that George Lucas explores are very much rooted in the here and now. Bortolin takes readers on a journey like no other—into their own hearts, minds, and spirits."—Jeff Cioletti, producer/director, *Millennium's End: The Fandom Menace*

"An interesting read that makes Star Wars more profound and Buddhism more accessible."—*Eastern Horizon*

"This book will appeal to Star Wars fans, to fellow Buddhists looking for insights from popular culture, and to people who are just curious about Buddhism."—*Saga Journal*

"Bortolin's pleasant humor and simple directness are immensely enjoyable and thought provoking."—Robert A. Johnson, author of *Living Your Unlived Life*

"Whether you are a fan of Star Wars or not, whether you are a newcomer to Buddhist thought or a long-time practitioner, Bortolin's light yet richly rewarding approach provides a fresh perspective that should encourage deeper thinking and practice."
—Frank Jude Boccio, author of *Mindfulness Yoga*

"A clear and clever introduction to Buddhism and an important contribution to the lexicon of modern Western Buddhist studies. The book draws an arc of meaning and wisdom across the centuries from Deer Park to the pinnacle of twenty-first-century pop culture."—*Ashé Journal*

THE DHARMA OF STAR WARS

THE
DHARMA
OF
STAR
WARS

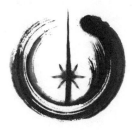

MATTHEW BORTOLIN

Wisdom

Wisdom Publications
199 Elm Street
Somerville, MA 02144 USA
wisdompubs.org

Library of Congress Cataloging-in-Publication Data
Bortolin, Matthew, author.
   The dharma of Star Wars / Matthew Bortolin.—Second edition
      pages cm
   Includes index.
   ISBN 1-61429-286-8 (pbk. : alk. paper)—ISBN 978-0-86171-828-3 (ebook)
   1. Religious life—Buddhism. 2. Star Wars films. I. Title.
   BQ5405.B67 2015
   294.3'367914375—dc23

                                2015011378

ISBN 978-1-61429-286-9   ebook ISBN 978-0-86171-828-3

19
5   4   3

Cover design by Philip Pascuzzo. Interior design by Jordan Wannemacher. Set in Adobe Garamond Pro 11/1/15.

Wisdom Publications' books are printed on acid-free paper and meet the guidelines for permanence and durability of the Production Guidelines for Book Longevity of the Council on Library Resources.

✪ This book was produced with environmental mindfulness. For more information, please visit wisdompubs.org/wisdom-environment.

Printed in the United States of America.

MIX
Paper from
responsible sources
FSC
www.fsc.org
FSC® C011935

Please visit fscus.org.

May the merit of this work benefit all beings.

TABLE OF CONTENTS

PREFACE

"Hokey religions and ancient weapons are no match for a good blaster at your side."

—HAN SOLO IN *A NEW HOPE*

What is the Dharma? And what in Sith spit does it have to do with Star Wars? Well, if you're like me, the Dharma has everything to do with that glorious galaxy far, far away.

The Dharma is the Buddhist teachings that point to the true nature of reality. Like an X-wing targeting computer that zeroes in on the bull's-eye, the Dharma isn't the target, the truth, itself; it only aims us in the right direction. That's because the true nature of reality isn't something that can be understood through words or concepts—it's the way your life is right now, free from the confusion of hokey religious beliefs, philosophical ideology, and Sith sophistry. The Dharma directs us to the truth of reality, or heart of real life. And my life has (almost) always been about Star Wars.

Like everybody and (nowadays) his mother, I grew up with Star Wars. The "Early Bird" figures, Death Star playset, Chewbacca's bandolier strap figure case—I played with all that stuff (and still do!). My earliest memory is the Star Wars logo slamming against the star-flecked blackness of my local theater's big screen. My dad whispered the crawl in my ear as it rolled passed, and I was hooked—Star Wars would forever be my life. If you cut me open, I bleed X-wings and lightsabers.

I came to process my experiences through my understanding of Star Wars. My interpretation of its myth colored the way I viewed everything from relationships to politics. My feelings of longing and boredom are always accompanied by John Williams's music and twin suns setting on my mind's horizon. Star Wars occupied my every waking minute. It was also my first experience with the Dharma, although I didn't know it at the time. "To me, Yoda is a Zen master," commented *The Empire Strikes Back* director Irvin Kirshner during filming. Zen is one expression of the Dharma, and Yoda did indeed say very Zen-like things. He tells Luke, "Do or do not. There is no try."

Most of us don't do, we try. We try to clean the floor, try to work at ILM, try to put the ship on the land—try to realize the truth of reality. Trying always implies a goal, an end result that doing leads to. We push through the doing to get to the goal. But the thing is, almost every second of life is doing. Goals can be achieved, but in a flash they're gone and we immediately turn our attention to the next goal, to the future, the horizon—never our minds on where we are, on what we are doing (to paraphrase Yoda). And before you know it, twenty, thirty, sixty years fly by and we've spent almost all of our lives pursuing goals that pretty much exist only in our heads.

Realization of the true nature of reality can't come from trying because trying suggests you already have an idea of the truth that you're aiming for. The concept of the truth is never the truth itself. You must put aside trying and do—fully engage in the present moment—then the truth beyond concepts will be revealed. This is called living a realized life.

There is a story I think Yoda would appreciate about a Buddhist student asking his master to explain the secret of the Dharma. When asked, the teacher answered, "Have you finished your breakfast?" Confused, the student stammered that he had. The teacher replied, "Then go wash your bowl."

Like trying to achieve a goal, the student is trying to grasp the meaning of Dharma intellectually. But the Dharma isn't interested in concepts. It's pointing us to concrete reality and encouraging us to live a realized life. We can't do that with our intellect. We have to do that by doing. By Force levitating the X-wing; by washing our bowl.

We live much of our lives in our head juggling two or more things at once. We try to puzzle out meaning and form conceptual frameworks that give purpose to our actions. This is understandable—it's part of being human. But to live a realized life we have to move past concepts and do what we are doing. Life isn't a goal we achieve or an idea we grasp. Life is what's happening right now.

"Do or do not" and "Go and wash your bowl" are clear directives to live a realized life. We do what we are doing or we don't. Trying resides in the realm of ideas.

Why is this important? Or in the grumpy words of Harrison Ford whenever he's asked about Star Wars, "Who cares?" Well, the reason I care is because life can only be lived in this instant and truth can be understood only in the present. I can also tell you when your mind is unencumbered by abstractions and your happiness isn't dependent on achieving goals, your life and the lives of those around you are simply better. And that's extremely important.

Hokey religions can't save us. Ancient weapons won't tame our minds. Like Han's blaster, the Dharma is immediate and practical. It isn't interested in simple tricks and nonsense. It's about your real life: bills, meetings, broken-down space freighters, and bowls that need cleaning.

If you want to know the truth, Buddhism urges you not to let time slip by. Life is short and death can come at any moment. So shoot first. Eat your breakfast. Wash your bowl. Don't trouble your life with abstractions. Just do. Then you will truly see what life is all about.

This new version of *The Dharma of Star Wars* is the equivalent of a Star Wars Special Edition. Unlike its movie counterparts, however, this book is more than CGI embellishments and shoehorned additions. It's a thorough examination of what the Force can teach us about Buddhism, and what Buddhism can teach us about the Force.

So strap on your lightsaber…or maybe don't. These pages will reveal only what you take with you.

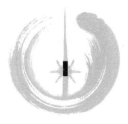

JEDI MINDFULNESS
AND CONCENTRATION

"Don't center on your anxieties, Obi-Wan, keep your concentration here and now where it belongs."

"But Master Yoda said I should be mindful of the future."

"But not at the expense of the moment; be mindful of the living Force, young Padawan."

—JEDI MASTER QUI-GON JINN AND
OBI-WAN KENOBI IN *THE PHANTOM MENACE*

The Star Wars saga begins with mindfulness and concentration. Jedi Master Qui-Gon Jinn reminds Obi-Wan, his Padawan, to be present and to keep his focus on the here and now. Qui-Gon's advice is good. It sounds like something you might hear at your local Zen monastery or Buddhist center. Being attentive to the present moment, rather than centering on what might happen later, is as important to Buddhists as using the Force is to Jedi. Mindfulness and concentration are the basis of Buddhism—and the foundation of the Jedi arts. These two practices are necessary to break free from mental hang-ups and constricting worldviews. And they are vital to waking up to who you are—to seeing your true nature and the truth of reality. "Waking up" isn't an intellectual endeavor. It's not a nugget of knowledge you can add to all that Star Wars trivia you've got crammed between your lekku. Insight into your true nature comes from living the realized life, from bringing the spirit of awakening to everything you do. The spirit of awakening could be another name for mindfulness. It's said that mindfulness is the energy that shines light on all things and everything we do. Mindfulness helps us see through our wrong perceptions and fears, and drop regret and worry. Mindfulness produces concentration, which leads to insight into the true nature of reality.

The way Qui-Gon uses the word "concentration" and the way Buddhists typically use it has a special meaning. We normally think of concentration as thinking about something really hard. That's not how Qui-Gon (and Buddhists) use the word. He isn't telling Obi-Wan to think about the present moment. He's not really talking about thinking at all. He's talking about fully engaging in the immediate moment at hand, without trying to describe, label, add, or subtract anything from it.

As Han Solo told Chewbacca when the Wookiee asked him how he's supposed to fly the *Millennium Falcon* at a distance but not look like he's trying to keep his distance: "I don't know," Han shouted. "Fly casual." Concentration is simply doing what we're doing. When we think about what we're doing, everything becomes contrived—it's impossible to be casual.

Mindfulness is awareness, attention, alertness. It's the opposite of spacing out or living forgetfully. There is a Zen expression: "If we live in forgetfulness, we die in a dream." Dreams can be lovely things (unless they're the nightmares of Anakin Skywalker), but dreams aren't real life. They're like the Ewok trap with succulent meat that Chewie triggered in *Return of the Jedi*: they entice us with the promise of happiness, but when we reach out to grab them—wham—we're suddenly the main course in a furball feast.

Yoda tells Luke that he has spent his entire life looking to the future. The future is a dream. It's that place beyond the horizon where we believe happiness exists—once we finish with this or achieve that. If we live like this, we'll just fall from one trap into another. The Buddhist practices of mindfulness and concentration are a wakeup call to cut ourselves free from the world of dreams and fantasies and come back to the only place we can live life and experience happiness—right now.

That's not the way we usually live though, is it? If you're like me, you probably tend to imagine that happiness comes later, like when I get done doing this thing I don't want to do and can lie back with a cool cup of Jawa Juice and fire up my Netflix to *The Clone Wars*. The thing is, living in forgetfulness, or doing one thing while thinking about another, is a hard habit to break. When it comes time to enjoy some serious animated Star Wars action, it's difficult to stop thinking about the next thing you're going to do once the show is over. Ahsoka Tano could be turning the entire Jedi Order on its befuddled head, but I'm fretting about everything I've got to do at work tomorrow.

Mindfulness and concentration aren't just about diving in and fully living the present moment, though; they're also about waking up to the truth, seeing through stubborn views of right and wrong, and removing conceptual bonds that keep us from touching true happiness. Escaping your distracted mind, like escaping Detention Block AA-23, is a really big deal, not just for us but for everyone we interact with. Think about how one careless word, delivered in forgetfulness, can crush a person's spirit. And what could one thoughtful word or deed delivered with mindfulness do?

In *The Phantom Menace*, Qui-Gon was gassed, attacked by droids, nearly blown out into space, and almost crushed by a droid transport ship when Jar Jar Binks stumbled into his path. By the time he reached Watto's shop on Tatooine, his patience was as thin as Yarael Poof's neck. "Don't touch anything," he snapped at Jar Jar in a moment of distraction as the Gungan toyed with a device in Watto's shop. Jar Jar recoiled at the comment and reacted out of irritation. He flapped his python-sized tongue at the Jedi master. Later, when the pressures of finding a way off Tatooine were relieved by Anakin's podrace victory, Qui-Gon approached the boy's mother, Shmi, moments before he took him from her for forever (as far as she knew). "I'll watch out for him. You have my word," Qui-Gon assured her as he squeezed her shoulder comfortingly. Shmi was visibly grateful. Mindfulness made the difference between a careless word that wounded and a gentle touch that healed.

Qui-Gon told Obi-Wan to be mindful of the living Force. Being "mindful of the living Force" means recognizing that life isn't just happening to us. We are happening to life. We are contributing to this world that everybody shares. We can make it a better place if we keep our concentration here and now. If we live in forgetfulness, we'll just keep grumbling at people for being who they are. When we live in mindfulness, we'll know what needs to be done to calm fears and soothe worried minds.

In *A New Hope* Luke Skywalker races his X-wing along the Death Star trench preparing to fire the proton torpedoes that would destroy the Empire's ultimate weapon. Fiddling with his ship's targeting computer, Luke hears Obi-Wan Kenobi's voice, "Use the Force, Luke." Unsure of himself, Luke dismisses the command and returns to what he believes he should be doing: targeting his mechanical scope for the crucial shot. Then the voice speaks again, "Let go, Luke."

When we let go of the belief that what we need is outside of ourselves and outside of the present moment, we are able to rediscover our true nature and the strength and stability already present within us. Obi-Wan urged Luke to switch the targeting computer off and let go. Luke let go of the ideas he had about destroying the Death Star and he stopped thinking about velocity and targeting computers. He just did what he was there to do—make a one-in-a-million shot that would save the galaxy.

Obi-Wan talked about letting go even before the attack on the Death Star. Aboard the *Millennium Falcon* he ordered Luke, "Let go your conscious self and act on instinct." The reason we're so often dissatisfied is because of our belief in the "conscious self." This idea of the self rests on the notion that we, the subject, stand apart from the world, our object. As such we are always trying to blast away aspects of the world we don't like and target and acquire what we do. We're rarely at ease with the way things are right now. When we are at ease, the apparent distinction between subject and object, you and the world, falls away. When you "let go your conscious self," you come into direct contact with reality.

This may sound weird, difficult to achieve, or maybe a little delusional. In truth we are in direct contact with life all the time, we're just not aware of it—nor could we be.

I read once that ten million lightsabers are sold every year. That's a lot of black eyes and cracked teeth. Despite the injuries, lightsaber battles are fun—especially when you've got plenty of room to maneuver and can really get into it: you eye your opponent and react to her moves, or you go all Sith offensive and pummel her defense with a furious barrage. You circle each other, the plastic blades go *slap crack*, your pulse quickens, and dewy sweat pops out on the skin beneath your hood. You're not fighting with a plan. You aren't even thinking. When you step out of your own way and let the parries and attacks come naturally, you're acting on instinct—your conscious self forgotten.

This is getting into direct contact with reality. You are mindful, present, doing what you're doing. There is no "you," no "lightsaber," no "fight." There's no concept of a "conscious self" to get in the way. There's only the seamless whole of the lightsaber duel. At the moment of experience, we and the experience are one. It's only when the "conscious self" arises and we parse ourselves from experience that the direct connection with reality is broken. Then we experience our lives filtered through concepts.

Luke was one with the Force at that instant he fired the proton torpedoes into the thermal exhaust port. There was no distinction between his self and the target; there was just the experience. If he had not let go of conscious self, he would not have succeeded in his mission of destroying the Death Star.

By developing what both the Buddha and the Jedi call mindfulness, we can also let go of the concepts that separate us from directly experiencing reality.

The method for developing mindfulness is easy to understand, yet surprisingly difficult to put into practice. The practice requires us to focus our awareness on what is going on within us and around us at this instant; it requires us to be mindful of the living Force. When we read this book, we know we are reading this book. If our thoughts drift off to what we are going to eat for dinner, or what events we have scheduled tomorrow, or what we would do if we had Jedi powers, then we are not reading mindfully. When you are reading, focus on reading. When standing, sitting, or lying down, focus on standing, sitting, or lying down.

Being mindful and staying present with life as it constantly changes, rather than thinking one thing while doing another, is much more difficult than it sounds. We may try to comply with Qui-Gon's advice to keep our concentration on the here and now, but mindfulness and concentration are not light switches we can simply turn on. We cannot just decide to be mindful and be done with it. Mindfulness takes practice.

It is difficult to be mindful right out of the gate because many of us have lived in distraction for years and even decades. Yoda once observed of Luke, "Never his mind on where he was, what he was doing." His observation could easily be applied to us. Our minds are rarely in touch with where we are and with what we are doing. We have accumulated many years of living without mindfulness—doing one thing mechanically while thinking about another—and this habit of living distractedly has become ingrained in us.

In fact, the habit of living distractedly is so strong in many of us it has become like a runaway podracer pulling us along. We try to wrest back the controls, but the energy of the thing is too strong. We are swept away by the habit energy of distraction and carelessness, and before we know it we've crashed into the side of Beggar's Canyon, bringing hardship to ourselves and others.

It's nearly impossible to truly understand mindfulness based on a description in a book. So let's get an idea of what it means by trying it out. After you read these instructions, stop reading for just a minute or two and try it out.

- Sit upright and breathe naturally.
- Turn your attention to your breath.
- Try to remain attentive to your in-breath, from its beginning all the way until it turns to become an out-breath.
- Try to remain attentive to your out-breath, from the moment it begins until it turns to become an in-breath again.
- Simply rest your attention on the breath in this way, following the cycle of the breath for a few minutes.

- When you find you have become distracted, simply return your attention to the breath.

Now you have directly understood mindfulness of breathing. (Give yourself a Wookiee roar of approval!) I say "mindfulness of breathing" because mindfulness is always mindfulness of something. Just plain mindfulness doesn't exist.

Luke Skywalker learned mindfulness of breathing on his first visit to Dagobah in *The Empire Strikes Back*. While climbing up vines, dashing through the undergrowth, leaping logs and rocks, the young Jedi pupil, his master on his back, is being instructed on the dangers of the dark side of the Force. Luke's mind races with a thousand questions about the dark side: is the dark side stronger than the good side of the Force, how can he distinguish it from the good, and why can he not do certain things? Luke's questions come in such a rapid-fire manner that it is clear to Master Yoda that Luke has lost touch with what he is doing in the here and the now. Noticing this, and sensing Luke's mind was running away from him, he brings the lesson to an end. "Nothing more will I teach you today," Yoda says. "Clear your mind of questions." With these words, Yoda is inviting Luke to leave behind the world of questions, concepts, and ideas, and return to the direct experience of life.

Often when we have concerns about a future event or confusion about the way something works, our mind becomes lost in a labyrinth of questions, doubts, and plans. Aware of this tendency, Yoda stops Luke before he becomes bewildered, rather than empowered, by his education and training. By directing Luke to clear his mind of questions, Yoda is instructing the Jedi student to come back to the present moment—to return to his breath. Luke does as he is told and the conceptual web he's wrapped himself in almost instantly unravels.

Mindfulness of breathing is the practice of simply concentrating on the breath. We note that a breath is long or short when it's long or short. We simply note the breath; we don't try to hold it or force it; we do not alter its rhythm or change its volume. Don't hold on to the idea that breathing should happen in a certain way. Simply become aware of the way the body naturally breathes.

As you practice mindfulness of breathing you may discover that the podracer of the mind—the speeding train of thoughts—kicks into a lower gear and slows down. At other times the mind may rocket into hyperspeed, seemingly accompanied by the roar of cheering spectators. Sometimes the mind is just like that—a cacophony of voices and clatter. We do not practice mindfulness of breathing to produce one state or reject another. We practice in order simply to be present to our lives right now—regardless of whether it's chaotic or calm.

Mindfulness of breathing is like a droid restraining bolt that keeps us anchored to the present moment. Like Jawas trying to lure us from our homes and into their greedy clutches, habits of distraction and overthinking pull us away from the here and now. Mindfulness of breathing is the restraining bolt that keeps us from wandering away from the safety of the present.

Without the restraining bolt of mindfulness we can be swept away by ideas and emotions. But by making good use of the restraining bolt, we can avoid being swept away. We can just watch our emotions and thoughts rise up like a sandstorm across the Dune Sea. Sandstorms rise and fall; that is their nature. Emotions and thoughts are the same way. Because we have our restraining bolt of mindfulness, we don't get carried away by our inner sandstorm and so we do not act rashly, based on temporary feelings.

The Jedi practices of mindfulness and concentration help us to discover ourselves and the ways we create dissatisfaction and frustration. Whether you're sitting on a meditation cushion, on the toilet, or in the navigator's seat on a spice freighter, the practice is to bring mindfulness to everything you're doing. This may seem like a pain in the ass (after all, that's a lot of sitting), but when you're not juggling a million things in your head, life becomes far less muddled and far more open to peace and joy. This type of practice doesn't have an expiration date; it is a lifelong practice without a finish line.

When you live your life with the spirit of waking up to who you are, realization can come at any moment. The Buddha, who in our galaxy was the first person to talk about mindfulness, realized his true nature when he saw the morning star after sitting under a tree all night. Zen Buddhism is full of stories about people who woke up due to a teacher's gesture, a smack to the head, or the sound of a rock caroming off a stick. Bring mindfulness to everything you do and who knows, maybe you'll see the truth the next time you fumble with your lightsaber trying to pull off the famous Whirlwind of Destiny move.

Mindfulness is a method of observation, not a means of becoming a different person. We don't need to become anything, we need only observe our feelings, thoughts, and the world around us. Carefully observing the world in this way can produce insight into its nature, which in turn brings a deep sense of peace and liberation. True and impartial observation does not turn away from uncomfortable truths but sees both the good and the bad, the light side and the dark, with clear eyes. Throughout Star Wars we see the Jedi practicing mindfulness and concentration not only as a means to better understand the Force but also as a means of preparing to face the dark side within.

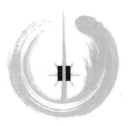

THE DARK SIDE WITHIN

"There's something not right here. I feel cold, death."

"That place...is strong with the dark side of the Force. A domain of evil it is. In you must go."

—LUKE SKYWALKER AND
MASTER YODA IN *THE EMPIRE STRIKES BACK*

The dark side of the Force manifests as anger, fear, aggression, and hatred. Master Yoda says in *The Phantom Menace*, "Fear leads to anger, anger leads to hate, hate leads to suffering." We all have the dark side within us. We can't run from it. Coming to terms with the dark side within is critical, not just for Jedi but for everyone. Fear is the first element Yoda mentions in the series of emotions that lead to the suffering of the dark side.

In *The Phantom Menace*, Qui-Gon faces fear in the intimidating form of Darth Maul. The Jedi battles the Sith in Theed, near the melting pit where laser force fields switch on and close like a wall between them. Instead of allowing his fear to overwhelm him, when the barriers go up between himself and Maul, Qui-Gon calmly kneels, centers himself, lets go of worry about what will happen next, and boldly faces the terror before him.

Buddhist practice is about accepting reality regardless of what it is. For many of us this means confronting frightening thoughts and mental activities that plague us. It's natural to want to flee from such things or to desperately try to destroy them, as Maul desperately wanted to destroy Qui-Gon. We fear being alone with our thoughts, and we fear making mistakes in front of others, failing at our jobs, and being publicly humiliated. We try to confront our fears by doing the things that frighten us. Little by little, we become acclimated to the things that terrify us and the fear seems to dissolve. But does it ever completely go away? Can we permanently defeat fear?

Darth Maul once said, "Fear is my ally." Fear is something the Sith use to weaken people, corrupt them, and bend them to their will. It's a very effective instrument. Who hasn't been rendered utterly docile by fear? When in the grips of extreme fear, don't you grasp wildly for someone or something to relieve you from your horrifying state?

But Qui-Gon wasn't subdued by the fearful power of Maul. He didn't even draw back and wait for Obi-Wan to help him once the laser doors swung briefly open. Qui-Gon wasn't afraid to face Maul alone because he had already seen the roots of fear in his own mind. He did not try to repress his fear, send it away, or ignore it like the inauthentic bully swaggering in front of him. Qui-Gon accepted his fear and didn't allow it to overwhelm him. Qui-Gon saw his fear for what it truly was, and that insight rendered his fear harmless.

The purpose of Buddhism is not to destroy fear—or the dark side. The things that terrify us aren't problems that we need to overcome. Fear itself is born out of misunderstanding the true nature of reality. It might have been more accurate for Yoda to say "Misunderstanding leads to fear, fear leads to anger," and so on. The roots of suffering will be covered later in this book, but for now it's enough to say that fear, and suffering in general, is unpleasant, but blasting it with turbo lasers or hiding under Imperial stairwells is not the solution.

We need to learn from Qui-Gon's example. Buddhist practice isn't a self-help regimen to take us from an undesired state to a desired one. Practice is about facing yourself right here, right now, and opening your eyes to the truth of who you are. That's what Qui-Gon did. Then, when it was time to re-engage Maul, fear couldn't push him back or cripple his ability to slap sabers with the zealous Zabrak. (Fat lot of good it did him—no son of Dathomir goes down that easily!)

Sometimes the dark side within can overwhelm us. We only need to look at Anakin and his slaughter of the Tusken Raiders in *Attack of the Clones* to see how entangled the dark side and suffering are. Anakin was overcome with grief when his mother died—an understandable and appropriate reaction. But his grief becomes hatred for her murderers and drives Anakin to slay them all, "not just the men, but the women and the children too."

We might imagine that acting out our anger will free us from it, but in Anakin's case his rage was not quelled by his action but intensified by it. Anakin failed to mindfully care for his sorrow and instead he allowed himself to be consumed by it. This begot the dark side, magnifying the suffering within him. Later, we see his suffering continues to grow when, at the Lars homestead, he confesses his actions to Padmé. Anakin is overwhelmed with misery. He explodes, throws a tool, and screams wild accusations before finally breaking down and weeping.

We cannot dispel suffering by acting on our anger or throwing a tantrum. In fact, the very effort to expel suffering is itself just another kind of suffering. We can lessen the intensity of our suffering by facing it with clear mindfulness so it does not overwhelm us as it does Anakin.

No matter what you're feeling right now—angry or calm, happy, sad, or indifferent, like a Sith or like a Jedi—it's just the way it is. And this particular moment couldn't be any other way. This is exactly how life is at this moment. Wanting, hoping, and wishing in vain for the present moment to be different than it is right now is what Buddhists call suffering.

The Buddha said, "I teach only suffering and the cessation of suffering." He was not interested in abstract philosophical theorizing that did nothing to change our lived experience. He refused to answer metaphysical questions or to entertain idle speculation. He directed people back to themselves and to the problem of suffering.

Suffering is a fact of life. It boils down to dissatisfaction with the way our lives are right now, driven by the constant search for what we think will make us happy only to discover after we get it that it wasn't the droid we were looking for. And then we're compelled to "move along" to the next thing…and the next—spinning in circles like hapless Stormtroopers, endlessly searching but never finding what we seek.

The previously presented practices of mindfulness and concentration help us to recognize the pattern of futile searching and to see through the suffering it creates. Living fully in the present moment as Qui-Gon recommends, we can observe the causes and conditions that give rise to longing and dissatisfaction. When we look closely, we begin to realize that our own previously unexamined views, beliefs, attitudes, and habits are what cause us to suffer. Mindfulness allows us to see how we Jedi Mind Trick ourselves into suffering.

In *Attack of the Clones* Anakin is struggling to accept the way things are. He is angry over his mother's murder and angry at himself for massacring the Sand People. He can't accept his own feelings even when Padmé reminds him that his feelings are natural.

"I'm a Jedi," he growls. "I know I'm better than this."

Anakin's anger in that scene is perfectly understandable. But Anakin believes he shouldn't feel anger. His idea of being a Jedi is that he should always be calm, serene, and detached from mundane human emotions.

"To be angry is to be human," Padmé says.

Anakin's idealized image of the Jedi puts him at odds with his own humanity.

The goal of Buddhist practice is not to rise above our human nature. Buddhas are not serene saints that glide atop clouds and peer pityingly down at us fools as we struggle with our out-of-control emotions. Buddhas are people who deeply understand the truth about ourselves and the world we live in, and attain great peace from this knowledge. Taking up Buddhist practice is about seeing ourselves and the world for what they are in this moment, and accepting them. Life can't be any different than it is in this moment. We accept or we struggle.

Acceptance doesn't mean that we should be complacent and vapidly watch as Sith Lords massacre their way to power. There is nothing complacent about Buddhist practice. Instead, acceptance means taking genuine stock of the facts of our situation: we don't waste time wishing things were different or telling ourselves they should be. Before we can improve a situation, we must first accept it for what it is.

Anakin's anger is painful to him. He doesn't like it. But this pain is not necessarily suffering. From the Buddhist point of view, suffering is not the pain one feels from an emotion, injury, or loss; real suffering is the belief that we shouldn't feel what we feel. Suffering happens when we can't accept reality—when we say that our human feelings are beneath us.

Anakin turned to the dark side because he feared losing Padmé. Fear of losing a loved one is understandable. But Anakin could not recognize or accept his fear. When we cannot clearly see or accept what is, we cannot work to change it. Anakin shoved his fear aside and blindly pursued a power beyond human (and Jedi) nature. Although his quest for power was born from compassion, it was consumed by fear, and that fear eventually overpowered him. Anakin fell to the dark side and a life of bitter suffering.

We need to accept suffering and befriend it. We must be willing to suffer, to be bored, sad, or afraid. Buddhist practice is an opportunity to bear witness to these unpleasant feelings, not to suppress them. By bearing witness we recognize each moment for what it is. This is how things are at this moment and that's not a problem. When we learn to engage each moment with acceptance, with each moment we are a bit more free. Then we gain freedom from our suffering.

To recognize that suffering is an undeniable fact of life doesn't mean that we agree with C-3PO's grouse that "We seem to be made to suffer. It's our lot in life." It is not our lot in life, because there is a way to establish a new relationship with suffering, one in which suffering doesn't seem so unbearable.

Suffering comes in many different forms, but there are a few basic types we can learn to recognize. A major class of suffering revolves around change. Life is perpetually changing. Because of this we constantly find ourselves encountering things that we like and things that we don't like. We hate getting older because youth is fun and death is scary. We're excited when we buy the Episode I COMMTECH Reader, but we get annoyed when the blasted thing doesn't work. Even when something good happens it later passes away. This is the impermanent nature of life.

After Luke Skywalker destroys the first Death Star in *A New Hope*, the rebels in their hidden fortress are elated. Not much later, however, the joy turned to fear as the Empire struck back and the small band of freedom fighters had to scurry into frozen hidey-holes on Hoth. Being stuck with something you hate, like a hollowed-out ice cube for a secret base, is an example of suffering.

Another form of suffering revolves around frustration. When we are forced to be in a situation we don't like or if we can't do what we like, we get frustrated. In *Attack of the Clones*, Anakin Skywalker feels smothered by his exacting master. He accuses Obi-Wan of hindering his progress as a Jedi and even implies that the older Jedi is to blame for his mother's death. Anakin is frustrated because he's not able to do what he wants to do and he cannot entirely control events in his life. That's what he felt the dark side had to offer: the power of personal control.

We also create suffering by playing the "should game": we tell ourselves we or the world should be different. We think we should not be the way we are or the world should not be as it is. We tell ourselves we should be better people and should not be such screw-ups. "I should be kinder, calmer, and more generous." This is the way I typically play the should game. Despite good intentions, when we start playing the should game we make our lives into a struggle. We struggle against ourselves. We judge and criticize ourselves.

Suffering is not always catastrophic or life changing; it can also be quite subtle. It can be nothing more than a pervasive feeling of restlessness, dissatisfaction, anxiety, and angst. The meandering search through life that leads us from place to place, job to job, partner to partner, hoping to find the missing element that will make everything as it should be is a type of suffering too. Dissatisfaction with the here and the now—the feeling that our happiness will occur sometime in the future, perhaps when we have completed school, gotten married, or raised our children—is a subtle form of suffering.

But malaise, the should game, pride, and self-criticism are not things we try to banish from our psyches. They aren't evil agents of the dark side that we must set out to destroy. They are merely aspects of ourselves that we must become mindful of, as Qui-Gon instructed Obi-Wan. The Jedi practice of mindfulness and concentration shares much in common with the ancient Greek maxim "Know thyself." When we know ourselves we understand the source of our dissatisfaction, and knowing this eases a great amount of our frustration and self-hatred.

To understand and free ourselves from suffering we must first recognize it. Following Qui-Gon's advice and being mindful in our daily life allows us to be aware of the presence of suffering as it manifests. So often we want uncomfortable experiences to be over so we can get to the next moment, one we imagine will be better. The practice is to recognize that we want things to be different. That's okay. We must first acknowledge our present experience and our feelings about it.

For instance, we may notice that frustration arises in us as we wait in an interminable line to get into the next Star Wars movie. (Considering modern conveniences like online ticket reservations and select seating, maybe I'm dating myself, but being a Star Wars fan is about waiting in line, dammit!) When we are unconsciously frustrated, that feeling sweeps us deep into suffering. Our jaw clenches and muscles tighten. We begin to find the people around us annoying. The kid playing in the queue grates on our nerves. We create a lot of suffering in the line because we just want the waiting to be over and the lightsaber dueling and starship battling to begin.

Recognizing our state of mind—in this case frustration—can stem the tide of suffering. Not recognizing our state of mind is like running around with a blast shield over our eyes—we are bound to get hurt and hurt others. When we recognize that we are frustrated and that our frustration is coloring our experience, it is like lifting the blast shield that has been blinding us from our eyes. Once we are able to clearly see what is happening, we are better prepared to act and respond to action appropriately.

Even if we recognize our state of frustration, we may try to bury our "feelings deep down." We don't like negative feelings like frustration any more than we like waiting in line. But repression just deepens our discontent. It would be wiser to approach our difficult mental states with an attitude of acceptance. It's okay that we become frustrated. Frustration, anger, hatred, and sadness are all part of life. We cannot avoid or dispel them. It isn't merely the presence of mental states like this that causes suffering; our aversion to them does. Trying to suppress, run from, or ignore frustration is simply a waste of time (and potentially a cause of more intense misery). If we accept the presence of frustration we gain insight that can free us from habits and perspectives that breed dissatisfaction.

We begin by looking deeply into our minds. Looking deeply means to investigate our frustration. We look to see the causes and conditions that have given rise to it. We don't think about why we are frustrated or psychoanalyze ourselves; we simply become quiet and sit with our current state of mind. Like Qui-Gon says, "Feel, don't think." This is what Anakin fails to do after the death of his mother. His attachment to the way he wanted things to be and his failure to prevent them from being otherwise overwhelms him—and he ends up massacring the Tusken Raiders.

Unlike Anakin, we can save ourselves from regrettable actions by looking deeply. When we were waiting in line, way back when, to see *The Phantom Menace*, we had plenty of opportunity to examine frustration—sometimes days…and bitter nights…exposed to the elements on the unforgiving pavement outside the theater where passersby heckle and Trekkies dressed like Spock tell us line-waiting is illogical. It's not always pleasant, I can attest. But at such times we can take notice of the current of beliefs that flows just below our frustration. We move past the *shoulds* and *shouldn'ts*, the repression and rationalization, and come to a quiet place where we see the root of our frustration. Seeing the root of suffering produces insight.

Insight into the source of suffering allows us to establish a better relationship with it. We cannot force insight to happen. Mindfulness, recognition, acceptance, and looking deeply provide the conditions that allow insight to happen naturally. When we see suffering for what it is, we understand how we ourselves create it. More often than not it is our perspective—the views we hold about how we should live—that creates suffering. Perhaps we think we should be living "big experiences"—climbing mountains, swimming with Nautolans and Mon Cals, or becoming "enlightened." Waiting in line, we believe, is tedium, and we're pissed we have to wait when life (or Lucasfilm or Disney) requires us to wait. Reality just isn't lining up (pun!) with our dreams of how life should be. Our limited perspective, our beliefs and expectations, prevent us from seeing how perfect everything is at this very moment.

Recognizing, accepting, and looking deeply into suffering is not always easy. Sometimes suffering can be much more elusive and darker than feeling frustrated in line. Other times suffering can be too painful to look at. For many of us there are aspects of ourselves that we don't want to know and that we would prefer did not exist.

Anakin suffers in *Attack of the Clones* when he cannot accept his failure and blames himself for not saving his mother. When we are confronted by our own failures and weaknesses we usually do our best to avoid them. We find ways to distract ourselves by turning on the television, broaching idle conversation, or drifting into fantasy. Such diversions help us to forget our worries, but they can't bring us the type of freedom from suffering necessary to be true happiness. We only find such freedom when we are willing to accept our suffering and take the time to carefully examine it.

When the Buddha looked deeply into his suffering he

discovered that it had no external cause but was the product of his own misunderstanding and attachments. We typically see other people, organizations, or events as the sources of our suffering. We think "if only" the world would conform to our ideals we would be happy. So we try to remake our friends and our family, or do away with the things we don't like. But this course of action can never be successful.

In *The Empire Strikes Back*, Luke believes Darth Vader is the source of much of the galaxy's problems. He thinks if only he can get rid of Vader the galaxy will be relieved of a great deal of suffering—that's why he didn't hesitate to attack the Dark Lord in the cave on Dagobah.

Let's recall that scene.

Luke has just finished a training exercise with Master Yoda when he turns a wary eye on a dark cave beneath a huge, black tree. "There's something not right here. I feel cold, death," he says in a halting voice.

"That place," replies Yoda, referring to the cave, "is strong with the dark side of the Force. A domain of evil it is. In you must go."

Yoda directs Luke into the cave to face the dark side residing there. The dark side is all the suffering in life: it is frustration, hatred, anger, and all the negative feelings and thoughts that come from within us. By going into the cave Luke is penetrating his own nature on a quest to recognize himself and the source of his difficulties. Yoda knows that if Luke can confront what lies within with courage and compassion, he will do much to overcome whatever hold the dark side has on him. But Luke makes the same error many of us make in our lives: he mistakenly believes his suffering comes from somewhere outside of himself. In this case, Darth Vader is the apparent source.

Out of the misty gloom of the cave's interior Darth Vader seems to appear. Luke ignites his lightsaber, and after a brief exchange of blows he defeats the Dark Lord of the Sith, separating his masked head from his body. Despite this apparent victory Yoda later calls Luke's experience in the cave a failure.

Luke fails because he was unable to recognize that the supposed source of his problems—the Darth Vader he faced in the cave—was in fact himself. When Vader's mask explodes it does not reveal the monster Luke had expected. Instead Luke's own face lies in its interior darkness. He hasn't killed Darth Vader; he's destroyed himself.

In *The Clone Wars*, Yoda has his own experience in the cave on Dagobah. Like Luke, he also confronts his personal dark side in the form of a vile little imp not too different from Tolkien's Gollum (with pointy green ears, of course). Also like Luke, Yoda chooses to battle his doppelganger, but he quickly learns he cannot defeat it with force of strength or will. Instead, Yoda chooses to embrace his dark side–nature. Embrace here does not mean "use"; it means to hold close as one would hold a wounded friend. By accepting his dark side, Yoda heals and transforms it.

Luke's experience shows us that imagining suffering to be something "out there" sets us up for failure and greater suffering. Suffering comes from within us. This was also the Buddha's crucial insight. To discover this for ourselves, we need to find time in our daily life to be quiet so we can recognize the beliefs and ideas that form the perspective that tilts us toward the dark side. Recognizing, accepting, and looking deeply into our own minds and seeing that suffering is a product of our perspective produces the insight that transforms bondage and suffering into freedom and joy. This practice of meditation to lift the shroud of the dark side is the training that we see the Jedi engaged in throughout the Star Wars series.

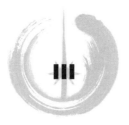

THE SHROUD OF THE DARK SIDE

"You and the Naboo form a symbiont circle. What happens to one of you will affect the other. You must understand this."

—OBI-WAN KENOBI IN *THE PHANTOM MENACE*

The Naboo and the Gungans are not the only creatures united in a symbiotic circle. All things are in a state of symbiosis, a state of interdependence with one another. In fact, the whole of reality itself is inclusively united. This fact is very difficult to see because the dark side clouds our vision of reality. In Buddhist terms, the shroud of the dark side is a misunderstanding that obscures the true nature of reality. This misunderstanding is the fundamental source of our suffering.

Misunderstanding is epitomized by the notion that creatures and things—Tauntauns, human beings, Wookiees, and even the stars themselves—have an independent existence separate from each other. The idea of an independent "self" is rooted in this fundamentally mistaken concept. Our sense of self-importance, fear of death, hatred of enemies, and even war spring from this basic misunderstanding.

The idea that we exist as independent selves is false because it ignores the true nature of reality, what Obi-Wan calls "a symbiont circle." Buddhists refer to this true nature as "emptiness." To be empty in this sense means to be empty of any unchanging, independent self.

We commonly think we are independent entities. We believe that we exist separately from others, but when we look deeply into what we actually are, we find that we are comprised only of elements that are not us. Our bodies are made up of organs and limbs that are not us, even our genes are made of bits of matter from our parents and ancestors, and at even subtler levels, we are made up of oxygen, carbon, and other atoms. Our thoughts are made up of what we have read, seen, and heard, informed by the culture we live in, the education we have received, and the movies we obsess over. We are not other than these things, but neither are any of them the self that we feel we are. We are empty because we are made up of and are interdependently related to things other than ourselves for our existence.

Consider a table made of Endoran wood. We know wood comes from trees. Looking at it we recognize this right away. But what we may not recognize is the existence of the forest, the soil, the rain, the sun, the lumberjack, the lumber mill, the carpenter, and many, many other things on which the table depends. Why would we? After all, a table is just a table. But if we trace the table back through its existence we discover that all these things played a part in its existence.

Even the full-grown tree from the forest on the moon of Endor from which the table was hewn was not really its beginning. That particular tree was just an arbitrary starting point; the tree itself had its own genealogy that stretches deep into the infinite past. The tree grew tall and strong over many years on a diet of air, sunlight, water, decomposed leaves, and other things. Without the air, sunlight, water, and decomposed leaves the tree could not have existed. The tree needed these basic elements to survive. Therefore, the air, sunlight, water, and decomposed leaves are integral to the existence of the tree. An Ewok may have grown old, died, and been buried near that very tree, which was coincidentally her favorite. As her body decomposed, it nourished the tree, and the Ewok, too, became a part of the tree. If we look deeply into the tree we can see her there.

Imagine we are on Endor and we wish to construct a table for laying out a nice spread of roasted rebels for dinner. We gather some friends, borrow a few tools from the furry natives, and fell a tree. We take the tree, shave off its bark, chop it up, shape it down, and produce a magnificent piece of furniture. The table would not have come into existence without our work, the axe we borrowed from the little furball locals, or the carpentry tools we used. It would not exist without the sun, rain, air, and decomposition process that helped the tree grow.

Looking at the finished table, it may be difficult to see all these different things in it, but they are there. If the rain had not fallen, there would be no tree, and subsequently, no table. Without the rain there is no table. If we had not had parents who loved us enough to feed us and keep us safe we would not have been there to cut down the tree. Without our parents there would be no table. Supposing by tradition we ate our meals on the ground, there would be no motivation for building a table to eat dinner on. Had all these conditions not come together in just such a way, the table would have never existed. What this means is all aspects of life, from the rain to the table to custom and tradition, are interdependent. And when we look deeply into their empty nature we find that they bleed into one another—that they exist in a symbiont circle.

If you lean three reeds against one another they can stand. Remove one and the other two fall. Take away the Ewok's axe or the food that gave us the strength to do our work and the chain of events that produced the table would not come to be.

The shroud of the dark side obscures the symbiont circle of interdependent existence. Not understanding the symbiotic relationship that is life causes us to suffer because it leads us to believe we are independent from the world around us. We may imagine we are separate from the forest, the air, and the earth. We think it does not matter that this forest is clear-cut, or that oil is dumped on the earth, or these toxins are released into the atmosphere. We may believe none of that will affect us because we fail to see that we are the air, forest, and earth too.

Looking deeply into ourselves we realize that we are entirely made of elements that are not us. Air, food, popular trends, and Jedi philosophy all come together to contribute to the person that I am. I hear Vader reveal who he is to Luke for the first time and I am suddenly a different "me" than I was a moment before. I look deeply into my Endoran table and see in it the seed planted by an Ewok hundreds of years ago. Understanding the world in the context of Obi-Wan's symbiont circle allows us to see past the surface of a thing to discover the whole universe within it.

If we were to look at R2-D2 through the shroud of the dark side, we would see nothing remarkable at all. He would simply be one of possibly millions of astromech droids in the galaxy. Droids of his make and model probably exist on every planet, in nearly every town and city. We might walk right past him, unaware of his presence—a bit of background machinery lumped in with every other unremarkable piece of equipment. That would be a shame, don't you think? It would be a shame because Artoo is a miracle: he is the entire universe in one squat, three-legged bucket of bolts.

In Artoo is Wedge Antilles—the X-wing pilot instrumental in destroying the second Death Star—who would not have been able to achieve his task had Bothan spies not discovered its secret location; those spies would not have been able to report their findings to the Rebel Alliance had the Alliance not escaped from the Empire's attack on Hoth, which could not have happened without C-3PO identifying the signal sent by the probe droid to the Imperial fleet; Threepio himself would not have been on Hoth had he been destroyed when the first Death Star was primed to annihilate the fourth moon of Yavin, which would have happened had two proton torpedoes not hit the space station's reactor system and set off a chain reaction; that one-in-a-million-shot could not have been achieved by anyone save Luke Skywalker; Luke would not have been in that X-wing had Stormtroopers not killed his aunt and uncle, and they would not have been killed had certain vital information not come, albeit unknowingly, into their possession; that information—the technical readouts of the first Death Star—would not have reached them had Princess Leia not been part of the scheme to deliver them to the rebels; Leia herself would not have been born had her mother not met her father. Padmé could not have met Anakin had she not fled to Tatooine, and she would never have reached that desolate world had her ship been destroyed by the Trade Federation blockade surrounding her planet, and that most definitely would have occurred had her ship's shield generator not been restored at the last second by a little astromech droid we know as R2-D2.

Perceiving the incredible web of causes and conditions, the number of lives touched and fortunes changed by one action of a single astromech droid we start to get a glimpse of just how deeply connected the universe is. The above example, however, touches only one linear chain of events. Stepping back from Artoo we begin to see that each point of contact—the rebel fighters, the Bothan spies, the Trade Federation—is an intersection between thousands of vectors of cause and effect that run in myriad directions. Drawing back further we start to get an idea of a complex web connecting all things.

Buddhists use the metaphor of Indra's Net to illustrate the web of interconnectivity between all things. The god Indra is said to possess an intricately wrought, jeweled net, which stretches infinitely in all directions. A multifaceted jewel is fixed at each node in the net, and each jewel reflects the jewels at neighboring nodes, which in turn reflect the jewels at their neighboring nodes, and on and on such that a reflection of every jewel in the infinite net can be seen in any one of its jewels. No matter which jewel in Indra's Net we look at, we would see ourselves and the whole of everything else reflected in it.

The Net of Indra is a metaphor for the web of interdependency that we discover when we look deeply into Artoo and discover proton torpedoes, Imperial probe droids, moisture farmers, economic embargoes, and the infinite number of things that comprise the entire universe—including us. None of these things exist on their own; they are empty of any real self because they exist interdependently. This is the insight of Obi-Wan's "symbiont circle."

The net of interdependence also exists within us. Each cell in our bodies is a culmination of all history and a container of infinite potential. Each cell is a product of our parents, ancestors, the food we have eaten, the air we have breathed, and the injuries we have endured. The history of a particular cell is limitlessly interwoven with the fabric of reality. The history of our cells is indistinguishable from our genetic ancestry. From time immemorial, that history has flowed like an endless river to this moment. We are the culmination and continuation of that flow. We are also the active potential for its perpetual flow.

In *Attack of the Clones* we discover that a single cell from the bounty hunter Jango Fett produced over a million clones. One cell of Jango's body, one cell of any human, contains the active potential for millions of lives! The enormity of sorrow, joy, love, and hate that can flow out of one cell is truly vast.

In the Star Wars galaxy a single cell from Jango Fett produced not only the clones but also the decimation of the Jedi Order, the fall of the Republic, and the tyranny of the Empire. The clones were vital to the plans of Darth Sidious (Chancellor Palpatine) to seize the reins of galactic power. They were at the center of a war that killed many Jedi and weakened the Republic beyond recovery. Without the clones the light of peace and justice in the galaxy would never have been darkened by the shadow of the Empire.

The rise of the Empire and the subsequent terror and domination over the galaxy can be traced back to that single cell! When we understand interdependence beyond concepts, we understand reality. The truth is Jango Fett is not separate from the Empire, the Clone Wars, or the destruction of the Jedi. All of those things were present in him long before he was first cloned. This is because each cell of his body—each cell of all our bodies—is intimately intertwined with everything.

It is natural to feel that we are separate from the world, as Boss Nass does. We commonly think, "This is me. That is you." We draw boundaries separating ourselves from one another and think that doing so protects us from other people's problems and troubles. But when we see through the shroud of the dark side we recognize our error. Boss Nass and the Gungans were forced to accept the inextricable ties they shared with their land-dwelling neighbors. The droid army of the Trade Federation brought war to the Naboo and soon after turned its destructive power on the Gungans. As the Naboo went, so went the Gungans. Because we are all inextricably connected, the suffering of others will become our suffering and their joy will become our joy.

If we fail to understand Obi-Wan's symbiont cycle, the unbreakable chain that links our suffering only ensures that there will be more suffering. To blame you for my unhappiness is one way I can cause you harm while simultaneously creating grief for myself—just like when Luke entered the cave on Dagobah and attacked the phantasm of Darth Vader, only to discover that it wasn't Vader he destroyed but himself.

Before Luke entered the cave he turned to Yoda and asks, "What's in there?"

Yoda says, "Only what you take with you." Luke took his lightsaber—a weapon that can maim, destroy, and split a person in two. His choice to carry the weapon indicates Luke's mindset. He saw reality as split in two: self and other, me and them, the good side and the dark side. This dualistic view of life is a view of the world seen through the shroud of the dark side. Because Luke couldn't see the symbiont circle, his interdependence with evil, he attacked the thing he wrongly identified as the source of the galaxy's troubles—the evil Darth Vader. Luke mistakenly believed something "out there" was the cause of his suffering.

Luke couldn't see himself in Darth Vader. He saw the

dark side as something that existed only apart from himself. But when Vader's severed helmet exploded to reveal Luke's own face, Luke realized the truth—the dark side was in him, and he was in it.

There is certainly evil in society—murders, kidnappings, and other horrible crimes, as well as the many subtler ways people can be cruel to each other. The typical conclusion is that these acts, when they are perpetrated by and happen to other people, have nothing to do with us. We believe they are the deeds of a deranged few and that their effects are limited to certain victimized individuals. But when we perceive the world as Obi-Wan does, we see that we are inextricably linked to the murderer and the murderer is inextricably linked to us. We are inextricably linked to the victim and the victim is inextricably linked to us. We share our community with everyone that lives in it. Buddhism asks us to look carefully at our lives to see how we contribute to violence and suffering in the world, and how we can promote reconciliation and goodness. Sometimes it just takes a kind word or gesture.

When Luke confronted what he thought was Darth Vader in the cave of the dark side, he was unable to see himself in the Sith. So he allowed his hatred of the dark lord to guide his actions. (Hey, it's hard to figure out all these deep Jedi truths about interdependence when you've done nothing but tinker with power converters and moisture vaporators all your life!) But it wasn't long before he discovered that hatred is never pacified by hatred, but only with kindness can hatred be pacified.

If we offer understanding and kindness instead of our anger and distrust to those we consider to be enemies, we will be able to pacify their hatred and our own. In a deleted scene from *Attack of the Clones*, Senator Padmé Amidala warned the Galactic Senate, "If you offer the separatists violence they can only show violence in return." She was right. What's more, just as hatred breeds hatred, so too does compassion propagate compassion.

We do not live independently in this world. We share it with all beings, both murderers and holy men, Sith and Jedi. We exist in unity with rivers, culture, and astromech droids. The practice of Jedi mindfulness and concentration allows us to part the shroud of the dark side to touch reality.

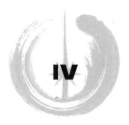

ANAKIN, LEIA, AND THE FIVE AGGREGATES OF SELF

"Master, moving stones around is one thing. This is totally different."

"No! No different! Only different in your mind. You must unlearn what you have learned."

—LUKE SKYWALKER AND MASTER YODA
IN *THE EMPIRE STRIKES BACK*

At the end of *Return of the Jedi*, a dying Anakin Skywalker looks on his son for the first time with unmasked eyes. "Now…go, my son. Leave me," he stammers with his remaining strength.

Luke's shock at his dad's charred marshmallow face morphs into compassion.

"No," he insists. "You're coming with me. I'll not leave you here. I've got to save you."

"You already have," Anakin says.

The notion that we are completely separate beings with permanent identities or souls is a false notion that shrouds our understanding of reality. Luke was no longer blinded by such conceptions when he saw his father's face for the first time in this scene. Where others saw only a man who was evil by nature, Luke recognized the good in his father. He knew that Vader's destiny wasn't predetermined.

Buddhism challenges our sense of a permanent, independent self, clearly identifying it as false. From the Buddhist point of view, all beings indivisibly interact with the whole universe and are part of the unified flow of life. What we commonly perceive to be our distinct individuality is in reality an aggregation of physical and mental elements.

An "aggregate" is a collection of various elements that make up a particular formation. Lemonade—a drink that we might expect to find being sold on the lush world of Naboo or refreshing a desert-parched patron in Chalmun's cantina in Mos Eisley—is a good example of an aggregate. Whether we find it on Tatooine or on our own world, lemonade is always an aggregate comprised of lemon juice, sugar, and water. We perceive lemonade as a discreet, uniform substance, but in reality it is made up of intermingled ingredients, each likewise interdependent. Every sentient creature—human, Wookiee, Jawa, or Mon Cals—is an aggregate of bodily and mental elements. Buddhists further subdivide mental elements, bringing the total number of aggregates that comprise a sentient being to five: (1) physical form or body, (2) feeling, (3) perception, (4) mental formations, and (5) consciousness. Each of these aggregates is of course comprised of various other elements. The physical body, for example, is made up of air, water, hair, bone, blood, skin, and many other things.

Each aggregate is also impermanent: it is never the same from one moment to the next. Because the aggregates do not endure, we cannot cling to any of them as an unchanging self or soul. Obi-Wan, Yoda, and Anakin might've been able to retain individual consciousness after death, but that's an impossible-to-imagine power we'll never have. The five aggregates are, furthermore, a part of Obi-Wan's symbiont circle and cannot stand independent from one another.

To better understand this whole five aggregates thing, let's take a look at Anakin Skywalker. The first thing we notice about Anakin is his body—the aggregate of "form." Once we've seen little, bobblehead Anakin in *The Phantom Menace*, we wonder why the dude has Sasquatch eyebrows in *Return of the Jedi* (I'm talking pre-DVD Anakin, when a pair of feather dusters sprout from a head that shouldn't have a strand of hair on it after being flambéed on Mustafar). The changes that Anakin's body underwent over his lifetime are quite evident. But these changes were not limited to the process of aging or scars from his duel with Obi-Wan. Anakin's body, as well as our own, changes continuously throughout its life. Our bodies are sometimes tired, sometimes energetic; healthy today and sick tomorrow; hair grows, teeth fall out, and weight is gained and lost. The body constantly changes, but much of that change is so subtle that we fail to recognize that our body right now is different from our body one second ago.

In his youth, the sunlight from Tatooine's twin suns lanced through the atmosphere to sear Anakin's exposed flesh, causing a chemical reaction that altered his skin, damaging some of his cells and infusing his body with vitamins. Years later, as Vader he stalked the halls of Cloud City, breathing its rarefied atmosphere. Each breath brought with it microscopic germs and particles into his withered lungs (hopefully not Ugnaught particles—bleah!), renewing his miserable life for a few seconds more. Anakin changed with the sun and he changed with the air.

Clearly we cannot survive without the sun or air. We also couldn't exist without a father and mother. If we examine the symbiont circle of Anakin, we find his mother Shmi and his daughter Leia. Leia came from Anakin's body. Leia cannot be separate from Anakin or her ancestors. She is an extension of them, a continuation of their genetic material. (But should Leia call Emperor Palpatine grandpa? He, along with Darth Plagueis, manipulated the midi-chlorians to create Anakin, right?)

To see the body as an extension of its parents, the food it has ingested, the air, earth, sunlight, and everything else is to understand that it is not separable from everything else. Our bodies existed in our great-great-grandmothers and they hold the presence of our great-great-granddaughters. So our existence is not trapped in our body. When the Buddha looked carefully into his existence he saw that it could not be found solely in the hands, arms, legs, feet, torso, and head of his body, but that it existed in his parents, the air, the sun—everywhere. From that point on he no longer feared death.

We fear death because we feel that we exist apart from the world around us and that our existence depends on our bodies. Fear of death is natural. It vanquishes even the most hardened. Take, for example, the Emperor's scream of terror as he plummets down the central core shaft of the Death Star to his death or Darth Maul's cowering mewl when he thought his master would destroy him in *The Clone Wars*. But while the shroud of the dark side hindered the Sith's understanding of reality, others were not so blind to the truth. Qui-Gon Jinn met death with no thought at all of himself, only compassionate concern for the galaxy.

Unlike Qui-Gon, we feel that when our body dies we will be reduced to nothing, and this causes a great deal of anxiety. But if we look deeply into our bodies we would see that they die and are reborn with each breath. The beginning of an inhalation is a kind of birth: fresh air enters our lungs and is drawn into the cells of our bodies, making them different in that instant than they were the moment before. By the time the inhalation turns to become an exhalation, we are no longer the same person who breathed the air in. Each cycle of breath is like a brief lifespan in which we are born and die. With each passing thought the mind is born and dies in the same way. When we look deeply at ourselves we realize we have lived through countless births and deaths without even knowing it.

Such insights may be of small comfort when we lose someone near to us. Obi-Wan wept as he held Qui-Gon, clutching his body after he died. (Little did he know that his master's brogue would be worming into his ear on Mortis and again later in the Star Wars saga. You just can't escape your teachers, I guess!) It was small comfort to me when I held my grandfather's hand after he passed, knowing that I would never again prune trees, pick fruit, or listen to seemingly endless stories with him again. Like Qui-Gon, he is gone, and I miss him.

But if we look carefully at Obi-Wan we find qualities of Qui-Gon present in him. Yoda pointed out this fact when he told Obi-Wan, "Qui-Gon's defiance I sense in you." Similarly, when I look deeply at myself, I see that my grandfather is not truly gone; he is in me. My grandfather no longer answers the phone when I call his house, but I can hear his voice when I am quiet and attentive, and I can see his presence in my thoughts and actions even now as I type these words.

Feeling, the second aggregate in our list, refers both to bodily sensations, such as hunger or pain, and to mental feelings of happiness, sadness, or indifference. When we observe our feelings, we see that they too are continuously changing. When she was held captive in the Death Star in *A New Hope*, Princess Leia felt anxious about her future and the hopes of the Rebel Alliance. She had seen Alderaan destroyed and didn't know what fate might have befallen Obi-Wan Kenobi and R2-D2—the droid who carried information vital to the survival of the rebellion. Her anxiety quickly changes to puzzlement when an undersized Stormtrooper rushes into her cell aboard the Death Star. The "Stormtrooper" removes his helmet and blurts, "I'm Luke Skywalker. I'm here to rescue you."

"You're who?" the Princess asks, both bemused and annoyed.

"I'm here to rescue you. I've got your R2 unit. I'm here with Ben Kenobi."

Her annoyance turns to guarded elation: "Ben Kenobi! Where is he?"

So in a matter of seconds Leia's feelings went from anxiety to confusion to irritation to joy.

Feelings, like the body, are always shifting. They change based on what our senses encounter and how we are conditioned to experience it. We experience pleasant, unpleasant, or neutral feelings whenever we see, hear, taste, touch, or smell something. The Buddha advised his disciples to be aware of their feelings as they arise in one context and fade away in another. Jedi Master Mace Windu advised young Anakin Skywalker in *The Phantom Menace*, "Be mindful of your feelings."

Being mindful of our feelings allows us to see that what we feel are also aggregates rather than distinct entities. Every feeling can be parsed into an object, the sense that encounters it, and consciousness of the encounter. All three of these are necessary for a feeling to arise. For example, to experience the joy of watching Star Wars, the movie must be playing, the eyes and ears must be able to receive information, and the mind must be attentive. Feelings of joy depend not only on objects that can be seen and heard, but on the eyes and ears that see and hear them, and the mind that appreciates them. The images on the screen, our sensation of them, and the mental state with which we encounter them interact with one another to produce the good cheer we feel watching Star Wars.

Understanding this, we know that our feelings are not ourselves. We cannot identify ourselves with our feelings; my love of Star Wars, however strong, is not "me." These things are products of countless elements in the world coming together one minute and fading away the next.

The Chewbacca that we see running across a TV or movie screen is part of us because he is the object of our perception. Perceptions are images that form in our minds as the result of sensory contact with objects in the world, like Chewie. Usually, whenever a sense organ makes contact with an object, a corresponding perception follows. At the moment of perception, subject and object are one. It's impossible to have a subject without an object. It's impossible to remove ourselves and retain Chewbacca. When the scene changes and Palpatine dominates the screen, our perception changes too—then Palpatine is part of us. (Suddenly, I'm feeling a diabolical urge for galactic domination.) And if you want to go crazy deep into the Force, Buddhism also says that we are part of Palpatine—in other words, the image of Ian McDiarmid in cloak and cowl on screen is actually altered by us, the viewer, as we watch him sneer at Luke.

In *A New Hope* Obi-Wan Kenobi leads his nascent learner, Luke Skywalker, in a training session aboard the *Millennium Falcon*. Luke uses his lightsaber to defend himself from small laser blasts that emanate from a hovering seeker-droid. Wishing to expand the lesson, Obi-Wan places a helmet on Luke's head that completely covers his eyes.

Luke is master of the obvious: "With the blast shield down, I can't even see. How am I supposed to fight?"

"Your eyes can deceive you," the Jedi explains, "Don't trust them."

The Buddhist tradition says, "Where there is perception,

there is deception." In other words, our perceptions are often incongruous with reality. And yet perception forms the basis of our sense of the world. When the Jedi met with Palpatine prior to the Clone Wars, they perceived him to be an honorable, or at least benign, leader. But they weren't interacting with the real Palpatine. They were deceived by their idea—their perception—of him, informed by his stature and place in the Senate. When they realized the full extent of their misperception, it was too late. The grandfatherly chancellor had played them like a space lute.

We must apply Jedi mindfulness to our perceptions to avoid being deceived by them. Perception can become an insight into the truth if we approach it mindfully. We see things more clearly when we see perception for what it is. Recognizing that perception can act like a blast shield opens our eyes to "a larger world."

Despite having stepped into a larger world in *A New Hope*, Luke still struggled with limited perception on Dagobah. Moving small stones around with the Force, he thought, was entirely different from lifting his submerged X-wing. Luke was trapped by dualistic thinking—dividing things into this and that, big and small, heavy and light. He didn't understand Yoda's assertion: "Size matters not."

Luke stands dejected at the edge of the swamp where only a small portion of his X-wing can be seen poking out of the murky water.

"Oh, no. We'll never get it out now," he moans.

Yoda, who has been calmly observing the situation, practically rolls his eyes at his obtuse student. "So certain are you. Always with you it cannot be done. Hear you nothing that I say?"

"Master, moving stones around is one thing. This is totally different."

"No! No different!" Yoda insists. "Only different in your mind. You must unlearn what you have learned."

As children our minds are relatively free of presumptions. We experience each thing, each event more as it is, without expectation. The youthful mind has not yet learned to categorize things, people, and feelings into familiar, preconceived packages. As a result a childlike mind is often able to touch life in ways that older, more knowledgeable minds cannot.

Take Obi-Wan Kenobi's experience in *Attack of the Clones* for example. Obi-Wan can't locate the planet Kamino in the Jedi Archives. Confounded, he approaches Yoda while the tiny Jedi master is training a group of Jedi Younglings. Upon presenting his dilemma to the group, a solution to Obi-Wan's problem becomes apparent: the planet had been erased from the Archive memory. It wasn't the older, more experienced Jedi that hit upon the solution, but a kid—the Padawan, J. K. Burtola. The child's mind, unlike Obi-Wan's, was less clouded by facts, knowledge, and presumption, and could more readily see the truth.

Presumption skews our perception of reality, giving us an impression that is entirely wrong. Luke's presumptions led him to perceive the rock and the X-wing as substantially different. He didn't perceive the rock as non-rock, or that the X-wing was in it. Yoda was teaching Luke far more than a feat of the Force; he was teaching him to see past perception limited by presumption to the truth. He was trying to unstick a mind that could only perceive a very small portion of reality.

Had Luke recognized that his perception was obscured, he would have guided the ship out of the water just as his master did. Instead he stood watching, slack-jawed, as Yoda parked his rig. Scooping his chin up off the dirt, he stammered, "I don't believe it."

"That is why you fail," Yoda sighed.

Luke is too wrapped up in what he imagines to be possible. The X-wing was lifted from the swamp and brought onto land, but he couldn't reconcile that truth of his perception with what he thought should be possible. He believes more in his ideas than he does in reality. Yoda is prodding Luke to drop attachment to his beliefs and see things as they actually are. He should have whacked him with his cane and said, "Your head, get out of and look." Luke couldn't believe that lifting a ship with the Force was possible, and yet there it was resting on the loamy shore.

The belief that his wife would die and his desire to save her drove Anakin Skywalker's transformation into Darth Vader. Anakin's conviction was so strong that he rationalized turning to the dark side in order to gain the power that he thought would save Padmé. Buddhists refer to the ideas and attitudes that initiate action and direct and shape one's character as mental formations. These influential ideas make up the fourth of the five aggregates of a living being.

Mental formations like attention, contact, or volition may be operative all the time, but others, like determination, mindfulness, or sleepiness, appear only under specific circumstances. Some mental formations are beneficial and others are harmful, and some are neither. Thinking is a mental formation that can be beneficial when our mind is clear and calm. At such times thinking helps us understand things better.

But at other times, thinking can be unhelpful if our mind is scattered or under a lot of strain—like Anakin's was in *Revenge of the Sith*. Unnerved by a dream he had of Padmé's death, Anakin took his worries to Yoda. Yoda told him, "You must train yourself to let go of everything you fear to lose."

But Anakin didn't follow this advice. Instead, Anakin's fear of loss developed into a determination to do whatever it would take to keep Padmé alive—even if it meant killing innocents and friends in order to attain the power he needed to do so. In Anakin's case the mental formation of determination became a compulsion.

In *The Clone Wars*, Anakin's determination to save his apprentice, Ahsoka Tano, when she was trapped beneath the rubble of the droid factory on Geonosis is also quite intense. It appears as if she is lost, but Anakin will not allow her to perish without a fight.

"Be at ease, Skywalker," cautions Luminara Unduli, a Jedi master whose apprentice was also trapped with Ahsoka.

"At ease?" an incredulous Anakin snaps. "We need to act now!"

But there was nothing for them to do—an entire mountain lay between them and their Padawans. Despite this fact,

Anakin mistook Luminara's calmness for resignation and accused her of abandoning their apprentices.

"You misjudge me," she explains. "I, too, care for my apprentice, but…if my Padawan has perished, I will mourn her. But I will celebrate her as well through her memory."

Luminara was not dismissing the hope of rescue, as Anakin seems to think. She is ready to act to save her Padawan, but at the same time accepts that some things are beyond her control—she has trained herself to let go of the things she fears to lose. In her case, acceptance and patience have become mental formations that guide her thinking and actions. Anakin has not cultivated those particular mental formations. Instead, his actions are still compelled by fear of loss and failure. Without having properly trained his mind he's still struggling to make "things the way [he wants] them to be," as he said in *Revenge of the Sith.*

Unlike Anakin, Luminara has cultivated wise and measured acceptance in place of blind determination that becomes compulsion. She makes this clear after the Padawans are rescued when she says, "It's not that I gave up on them, Skywalker. But unlike you, when the time comes, I am prepared to let my student go. Can you say the same?"

Luminara is unafraid of loss. Anakin is terrified of it. His annoyance and surly behavior during the rescue effort is an indication of how truly afraid of losing Ahsoka he is. This fear, fear of things turning out different from how he wants them to be, is the germ of the dark side. This type of mental habit is what compels us to seek power over the way things naturally are and to manipulate people, things, and events that we dislike. Anakin does not understand that accepting that some things are beyond his control is different from abandoning his friends. (This is the same mistake that Luke made when he left Dagobah in *The Empire Strikes Back*.) Luminara, on the other hand, is humble and realistic. She will do what she can, but, at the same time, accept what she cannot control.

Mental formations are the product of our upbringing, education, environment, and experience. Anakin's life as a slave, his "failure" to rescue his mother, and the Clone Wars all contributed to the mental formations that drove him to the dark side. Similarly, Luke's colorless life on a moisture farm, his massacred guardians, and the rebellion all contributed to the mental formations that drove him to an entirely different decision—a decision born of compassion rather than fear. Mental formations comprise an integral part of who we are as people, but nowhere in them can we find the real "self" that we innately feel we are. Like all of the other aggregates, mental formations can be further reduced into constituent parts and are subject to change, and thus cannot be relied upon as a foundational element of the self.

Consciousness, the last of the five aggregates in our list, is the fundamental basis for our sense of being. It is the ground upon which all of our mental formations rest. Like feeling, perception, and mental formations, consciousness is also influenced by contact with the world of phenomena. When the senses come in contact with something in the world, unless we are distracted or impaired, we are normally conscious of it. Once your eyes have seen these words you become aware of them. When your ears hear the ominous breathing of Darth Vader you become aware of his respiration (and no doubt fearful that some great evil is about to befall you). When a thought or memory sparks in the mind, you are aware of it. Consciousness is always aware of something.

In some philosophies and religions consciousness is considered to be the true self, distinct from form and everlasting. This seems to be the case for the Jedi in the Star Wars universe. Yoda pinches Luke and tells him, "Luminous beings are we, not this crude matter." But this is not so for Buddhists, who consider consciousness to be conditioned, just like form, feeling, perception, and mental formations. Our eyes and what they see are conditions without which visual consciousness would not occur. Our ears and what they hear are the conditions without which auditory consciousness would not occur. The imprints, impressions, and memories in our minds and the preceding moment of consciousness are conditions without which mental consciousness would not occur. Consciousness depends upon the world as much as it does upon the mind and body. And because it is conditioned, consciousness changes from moment to moment. Consciousness is thus a dependent and impermanent phenomenon, just as all the other aggregates are, and cannot be a reliable basis of the self.

Yoda implies that we can transcend death and live on, untethered to the body. A good deal of the Star Wars mythos rests on this notion that individual consciousnesses can carry on after death, teaching disciples, watching over and influencing events as they unfold. It seems that way, anyway, until Qui-Gon, as a ghostly, postmortem presence explains in *The Clone Wars* that his presence is a "manifestation of the Force." He is not separate from the Force, but part of it. "All energy from the living Force, from all things that have ever lived, feeds into the cosmic Force, binding everything and communicating to us through the midi-chlorians." he says, "Because of this, I can speak to you now." Consciousness, even in the galaxy far, far away, is an aggregate, a constitute part of the greater whole. It is not a reliable basis for the self—even hazy-blue Jedi selves.

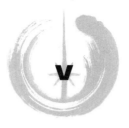

ESCAPING TATOOINE AND THE CAUSE OF SUFFERING

"Are you allowed to love? I thought that was forbidden for a Jedi."

"Attachment is forbidden... Compassion, which I would define as unconditional love, is central to a Jedi's life. So you might say that we are encouraged to love."

—PADMÉ AMIDALA AND ANAKIN SKYWALKER
IN *ATTACK OF THE CLONES*

Suffering does not arise without a cause. That cause is the action of grasping or rejecting various forms of desire and ideas as they arise in our mind. Desires and ideas (or mental formations like Anakin's hatred) are themselves not suffering, and they should not be seen as a threat. Suffering is not the feeling of fear, the desire for revenge, or the belief in the soul, it is attachment and aversion to those things—or any of a host of others. Suffering is the act of tenaciously grasping ideas about how things "should" be, views of what happiness is, blind convictions about what life is all about. Suffering happens when we fail to see each successive moment clearly and fully, and we become lost in ideas and desires that we believe are the truth of life. Simply put, attachment and aversion to ideas and desire produce suffering. We chase after what we like and run from what we don't. And we, like Anakin, never learn to "let go of the things we fear to lose."

Buddhist philosophers describe three types of desire that, when grasped or rejected, cause suffering. The three types are desire for things that are pleasant to experience, desire for something to not be the way it is, and the desire to have more or to be more. Desire for pleasure creates suffering because its demands for eternal fulfillment are continually frustrated by the impermanent, unsatisfactory nature of the world. In other words, things change. Nothing can exist eternally. Everything we cherish and hold dear today, we will have to let go of and be separated from in the future.

Artoo is a composite being: he is composed of separate elements. Not just gears and wires, but also the ice of Hoth, Wedge, and the Imperial fleet. A tree on Endor is also composed of separate elements: the rain, sunlight, soil, and Ewoks. As we've seen everything is interrelated, and therefore everything is a composite. Everything is made up of everything else—existing in a continuous cycle of transformation.

We have a tendency to cling to things that bring us joy or make us happy, hoping they will never leave us. A mother may not want to see her child leave to become a Jedi, a Twi'lek dancer may quake at the thought of her beauty fading, a Jedi may dread losing his wife. But the fact is all these things leave us. We cannot stop change any more than we can "stop the suns from setting," as Shmi Skywalker, Anakin's mother, says. All things are of the nature to pass away; we suffer when we do not release them. Like Jedi we must train ourselves to "let go of everything we fear to lose."

When things that bring us joy are gone we are left feeling hollow, and we try to fill up this hollowness with new things: Star Wars video games, jogan fruit, Corellian whiskey, Star Tours trips to Naboo. While each new thing can be a small joy, none provide us with lasting relief from that hollow feeling. They are all impermanent, and the contentment they bring today is gone tomorrow.

Please understand it is not the video games or drinks at the Outlander Club that cause suffering (we can surely enjoy them while they're here), it is the belief that they'll fill up our internal hollowness that creates in us a repetitive pattern of grasping, attainment, loss, and frustration. The Buddha taught that living beings, led by craving, rush about aimlessly like trapped rabbits. Caught in desires, we suffer over and over again. When we are led by our desires, rather than free to take them or leave them, we are caught in a cycle of obtaining and losing, pleasure and frustration—and we suffer over and over again.

Composite phenomena are not the only things that are impermanent; desires and beliefs are as well. If we take the time to watch our mind carefully we will see that desires rise and fall. Underneath them is profound peace.

In *A New Hope* Luke Skywalker could not accept living on Tatooine. He was bored and felt trapped there because Uncle Owen wouldn't sign his permission slip to join the

Academy. He longed to escape the drudgery of that desolate place to find romance and adventure among the stars.

This is an example of the second type of desire that produces discontent: desire for things to be other than they are. In its most basic form, this desire is an act of aversion, an act of turning away. Aversion is frustration with life in the here and now. It's the desire to be rid of a dissatisfying situation. It's an energy that doesn't accept life in the present moment but whines ineffectually about it instead of examining it carefully to see how to improve it.

Like Luke, many of us believe the grass is always greener on the other side of the galaxy, that Tatooine (or, specifically, this moment) is the source of all our problems and if only we could escape it everything would be okay. This is a negative perspective. Negative perspectives can be changed. Remember what Obi-Wan told Anakin: "You're focusing on the negative again. Be mindful of your thoughts." Qui-Gon echoes this sentiment in *The Phantom Menace* when he contends, "Your focus determines your reality." Focusing on all the things we find unpleasant creates an unbearable reality. But if you focus on what you've already got—then, hey, things aren't so bad.

Think of it this way: Happiness is not having your hand cut off by a lightsaber. When your hand is cut off, your arm hurts like hell, and you think, "Blast, I wish my hand weren't cut off! I could use that thing!" So if you have your hand then you aren't experiencing the pain of dismemberment, and you can still use it to meditate in a handstand, twirl a lightsaber, or pilot a podracer—and that's a lot to be happy about! Make sense?

Yoda reproaches Luke in *The Empire Strikes Back* because his mind was never focused "on where he was, what he was doing," but lost in dreams of adventure and excitement. "A Jedi craves not these things," Yoda says. That craving arises is fine. It is when a Jedi clings to craving that he suffers. And this will happen if the Jedi is not practicing living Force-mindfulness. When we are doing this, when we are mindful of our cravings, we can choose to act on them if we think they will benefit us, rather than be a slave to them and obey them whenever they yank on our collar chain (one of Jabba's favorite pastimes with his thralls).

Anakin Skywalker lost himself in his desire to save Padmé. The good man that was Anakin was destroyed, and he became Darth Vader. This is an example of the third type of desire—the desire to have more or to be more. Becoming is nearly the opposite of aversion: aversion is the desire to be rid of something; becoming is the almost blind quest to attain it.

Craving to be famous, to have authority, to be like Yoda are examples of this third type of desire. Buddhist practice, like Jedi training, is a path of self-awareness. The arts of mindfulness and concentration, and meditation too, are intended to help us get in touch with who we are. They aren't designed to turn us into someone else. We cannot become anything more than what we already are.

Attachment to the idea of becoming "the most powerful Jedi ever" or an "enlightened being" is a quick path to the dark side. The key is not "becoming" but rather "understanding." The more we understand ourselves, the more we feel comfortable with who we are. And who we are is who we're supposed to be. We don't need to turn ourselves into little green Jedi masters.

Buddhists assert that the false view of self is the root of our suffering. It can produce selfishness, hatred, and arrogance that can lead to conflicts between friends, families, and even nations and worlds. It can also lead to internal struggles with the dark side that, in Darth Vader's case, had galactic-scale repercussions.

Clinging to our sense of self can also produce little sorrows in our daily lives. Reflecting on how attached we are to ourselves, we find that we secretly harbor a great deal of egotism and insecurity. Our minds are constantly critiquing others, comparing ourselves to them, and angling for respect. One moment we feel we're better than the people around us, the next we feel we're not as good as they are.

Attachment to the idea that we should get only what we like and not have to deal with what we don't also causes us to suffer. An ancient Zen master once said that the Great Way (of the Buddha) isn't difficult for those unattached to their preferences. He went on to say that if we let go of longing and aversion, everything will be clear and undisguised. We all have preferences. Some of us prefer the original theatrical version of Star Wars; some prefer the Special Editions. Some prefer their Jedi to be laid back and cool, like Qui-Gon. Others prefer the more kick-ass variety, like Quinlan Vos. The old Zen master isn't saying that we have to suppress these preferences and be forever indifferent; he's simply saying that attachment to preferences, making our preferences into requirements for the world, obscures our view of the symbiont circle. We do not realize the truth, we don't accept the moment as it is, when we're caught up in own preferences.

Yoda eloquently displays letting go in *Return of the Jedi*: He has seen the galaxy fall from peace into chaos. He has witnessed the Sith take over and the Jedi all but disappear. He knows his life is ending and the dark side still holds sway over the galaxy. Yet he does not suffer from aversion to that new order. He does not suffer by desperately clinging to his ideas, his beliefs, or the five aggregates of self. He knows twilight is upon him and night will soon fall. He is able to let go and clearly see that whatever is subject to arising is subject to ceasing. "That is the way of things," he says, "the way of the Force."

In *Attack of the Clones* Anakin Skywalker reveals yet another form of attachment that can cause suffering—attachment to infatuated romantic love or the desire to "possess" another. Consider this scene:

Aboard a transport en route to Naboo, Padmé remarks to Anakin that it must be hard for him to have sworn his life to the Jedi. Anakin replies that it is indeed difficult because he cannot be with the people he loves.

"Are you allowed to love?" Padmé asks. "I thought that was forbidden for a Jedi."

Anakin's smarmy response is classic kitsch: "Attachment is forbidden...compassion, which I would define as unconditional love, is central to a Jedi's life. So you might say that we are encouraged to love."

Buddhism talks a lot about "attachment" as a kind of greedy clutching that creates suffering. But there's another type of attachment that does not lead to unhappiness. Attachment, in the psychological sense of the term, happens when we connect with other people and form friendships. Attachment in this sense is simply love—and it's not something any sane person would forbid (or ever could). Maybe this was what Anakin was attempting to argue, but it seems that the Jedi ban on attachment is meant more in the spirit of the old Zen monk's thoughts on preference: if you believe one person, thing, or place is what you need to be happy, you're missing the big picture and setting yourself up for a Death Star-sized measure of hurt.

Romantic love can be a problem when it's based on misperceptions and mistaken beliefs about the objects of our love. We can invest so much of our hopes and dreams into one person that we build a monument to them in our mind and fail to see that they're just human beings. Anakin does this the first time he meets Padmé in *The Phantom Menace*: he compares her to an angel—attributing a superhuman quality to her that she could never live up to except in his dreams. Padmé is just a person—imperfect, ever changing, and incapable of being any man's happily ever-after—and she shouldn't have to be.

So what was it about Anakin that made him so stuck on Padmé? She's much smarter than him and good looking and all, but, man, he murdered kids for her! Then again, maybe his villainy had more to do with him than her. Maybe his insane "love" came from growing up a slave and never really feeling safe and secure. He must have been under constant threat of uncontrollable, undesired change. At any moment he could pass from one slave master to another or lose his mother to a gambler's wager or simply have the peace of an idle moment ripped away. It is understandable that the moment he had something he could call his own he clung to it with the tenacity of a spice-junkie hoarding the last traces of glitterstim in the galaxy.

And then one day it happened. He escaped his slavery and became a Jedi-in-training. He quickly grew in skill and power, which when coupled with his natural flair for fixing things, led him to believe that nothing was beyond him. No longer would the things he loved be taken from him. He would make the world and nature bend to his will. He would carve out an enclave of safety and security that would encompass the entire galaxy so he would never have to experience fear again.

Instead of confronting fear within himself, as Jedi are trained to do, Anakin attempted to reorder the external world to his liking, purging everything that made him uncomfortable. As Darth Vader he used power, intimidation, and murder to insulate himself from fear. But no matter how powerful he became, he could never control everything. This must have made him very anxious underneath his cold exterior. So he felt compelled to continue with the dark side, because if he didn't, he'd have nothing but himself left—and that was far too terrifying a prospect to contemplate.

We have to be careful how we handle the dark side within us. Accepting its presence should not include indulging in it or seeking it out. Reifying unpleasant aspects of life can distort our views, perceptions, and actions. When seen through the shroud of the dark side, the problems that assail us in life look to exist on their own, out there in the world. We should be careful not to develop the habit of seeing the world this way. Like Yoda told Luke, "If once you start down the dark path, forever will it dominate your destiny. Consume you it will, as it did Obi-Wan's apprentice."

Anakin unwisely went too far down the path into darkness. His fear of loss and his fear of a world he could not control drew him into an interminable spiral of destruction.

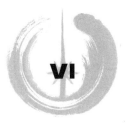

VI

DARTH VADER'S KARMA

"Remember, a Jedi can feel the Force flowing through him."

"You mean it controls your actions?"

"Partially. But it also obeys your commands."

—OBI-WAN KENOBI AND LUKE SKYWALKER

IN *A NEW HOPE*

In *Return of the Jedi* Darth Vader makes a decision that changes everything. He chooses to forsake the dark side and to destroy his evil master, Emperor Palpatine, thereby saving his son even as he brings about his own death. Yet Vader's decision was not solely his to make. In part, Vader is carried to that decision by life itself. Vader was born Anakin Skywalker, a slave on a remote world, who by chance met Jedi Master Qui-Gon Jinn. Qui-Gon began Anakin's Jedi training, an education that put him in a position to be tempted by the dark side and later, in the wake of the Clone Wars, led him to become Darth Vader. But something else happened when he met Qui-Gon; he fell in love with a girl named Padmé. He married Padmé, and they had two children, Luke and Leia. Years later it is Luke whose insight and compassion help awaken Anakin. And when the truth tears away the Sith scales from his eyes, Anakin finally acts for the good of others. He seizes Emperor Palpatine and saves his son's life.

Through Anakin's experience we can see that life is a vast web of cause and effect, conditioning all aspects of the universe. When we look at where we are right now we cannot say we got here all by ourselves. Whether in a prison or a penthouse, our upbringing, our education, even our nationality, all helped create our present status, personality, and state of mind. We cannot stand outside the network of cause and effect that is life. Rather, we are part of and conditioned by the perpetual movement of life.

Without the Emperor and his entire Sith legacy there would have been no threat to the Republic. There would have been no trade embargo of Naboo, no crisis in the Senate, no secession movement, no Clone Wars, and no destruction of the Jedi Order. Without the trade embargo of Naboo it is unlikely Anakin Skywalker would have ever found his way to the Jedi Temple, met Palpatine, and turned to the dark side. Had he never turned to the dark side he would not have battled his son. His son, in fact, would have never been born had he not met Padmé. And their meeting was contingent on the trade embargo of Naboo. Anakin needed the trade embargo, needed the Clone Wars, and needed his son to put him in the position to save the galaxy. Had conditions not come together in such a way for Anakin he may never have destroyed the Emperor in *Return of the Jedi.*

Seen from this perspective, Vader's act of killing the Emperor began long before Luke was born. It began before Anakin was born and even before Palpatine was born. Each of their lives and actions played a crucial role in setting up Anakin's heroic act, but they were all conditioned by the world. All actions, all thoughts are conditioned by what has come before them and what is occurring simultaneously with them. We can call this cause and effect—but that is not entirely accurate.

"Cause and effect" suggests a beginning and an end, with one thing clearly the cause and another clearly the effect, but there is no sequence that could be isolated and defined with a definitive starting point and an end. Life is not a two-dimensional timeline; it's multidimensional and conditioned from all directions. Everything has an impact on everything else. Consequently, life is, in a sense, guided by the interaction of conditions. Yet this gives only a partial, and overly mechanized, picture of life, for there is another factor we need to consider: human will and action.

Recall Luke's first training aboard the *Millennium Falcon* in *A New Hope.* Obi-Wan instructs Luke, "Remember, a Jedi can feel the Force flowing through him." "You mean it controls your actions?" Luke asks. "Partially, but it also obeys your commands."

We know from looking at Darth Vader's experience with the Emperor that *life* conditions us. When Obi-Wan says the Force "partially" controls our actions, it is like saying life conditions us. We are, of course, active participants in our lives. We are conditioned by the universe, but conversely, we condition it. Ideas, beliefs, salient issues flow through us from our friends, neighbors, world events, and the media. They become part of us, alter our thoughts and our actions, but we also add a bit of ourselves to them. Thoughts, feelings, and world opinion are both collective and individual. The collective contributes to our individual thoughts, feelings, and opinions; our individual thoughts, feelings, and opinions help make up the collective. The collective influences the individual, and the individual influences the collective. The two interpenetrate one another.

While life partially controls or conditions our actions, it is also influenced or "commanded" by those same actions; the Force obeys our commands. Luke's destiny in the original Star Wars trilogy appeared to have only two possible conclusions. Either he would do as Obi-Wan and Yoda had urged him to do and destroy his father, or he would turn to the dark side. Everything in his life propelled him to this fork in the road. Yet when he reached it he chose neither. Instead he cast his lightsaber aside; he did not kill, and he did not fall to the dark side. This act of will sparked something in his father that propelled him to make his own decision. And Vader's choice changed the galactic balance.

We live in a deeply interconnected relationship with all of life. That interconnection means you affect me and I affect you. Moreover, that interconnection means I affect *me*. The fact of impermanence reveals that we are never the same person from one moment to the next. Because of this, my thoughts and actions of today affect the "me" of tomorrow. Life partially controls who I am, but it also is conditioned by my will and my actions. Our willful acts and thoughts do matter—they can make the world a better place (for example, Vader's decision to save his son), or they can make the world a hell (Anakin's decision to turn to the dark side). It is our volitional acts, our will, that in Buddhism are called *karma*.

Karma is an intentional action or thought. It is the action or thought itself, and not the result of an intentional action or thought, as is sometimes believed. Reading this book is karma; the result one acquires from reading this book is called "karmic fruit"—the result of the seeds of karma coming to fruition. For there to be karmic fruit there must be intentional action or thought.

What we think or do in the present often depends on our perception of right and wrong. We want to do good, but the right course of action isn't always as clear as it appears in Star Wars—with the good on one side and evil on the other. "But how am I to know the good side from the bad?" Luke asks in *The Empire Strikes Back*. To which Yoda promises, "You will know. When you are calm, at peace." When we put aside our ideas of right and wrong and calmly accept things as they are, the right course will present itself. But it might not always be the "right" we think it should be.

Alone during his self-enforced exile on Dagobah, Yoda had plenty of time to reflect on his past. He might have blamed himself for his choices, his mistakes, and his failure to see what was really happening during and before the Clone Wars. He could have concluded that his isolation was deserved because past actions were so incredibly feeble and inadequate to prevent the takeover of the Sith.

It's true that Yoda bears some responsibility for the fall of the Jedi and the Republic, but the outcome of the Clone Wars was the result of the karma of far more than a single individual. Alone on Dagobah Yoda understood this to be true, but he also knew that the past was gone. He knew his actions in the present mattered most. He trained himself and prepared for the day that he would teach Luke Sky-walker to bring an end to the tyranny of the Sith.

Karma is about what you're doing right now. The past is gone; the future is only a fantasy. Here and now we can choose to perpetuate the mistakes of our past or stop them and take a new course. Good can be realized only in the present. Only when you are fully present here and now can you know what is the right thing to do right now.

Recall this scene from *Return of the Jedi*.

"You cannot escape your destiny," Obi-Wan tells Luke. "You must face Darth Vader again."

"I can't kill my own father," Luke insists.

"Then the Emperor has already won."

Later, as Luke stood over his fallen father prepared to destroy him, the Emperor was ecstatic. "Good! Your hate has made you powerful. Now, fulfill your destiny and take your father's place at my side!"

By this point Luke was a Jedi, he had seen through the shroud of the dark side. To kill Vader, as Obi-Wan wanted, would have placed Luke exactly where the Emperor desired him to be—at the Sith Lord's side. On the other hand, to let Vader live would have meant that the evil of the Sith would continue. Either choice would have led to the same result: the dark side. But Luke was not controlled by his past. In the present moment he was free to choose, and his choice saved the galaxy.

While our present state of mind is in large part based on our past karma, we shouldn't adhere to a doctrine of determinism and believe that everything that happens is simply fate. The idea of karma emphasizes the importance of human volition. And despite Luke's often-mentioned "destiny," the Star Wars saga as a whole seems to be in agreement with this view.

Luke made the right choice. He deactivated his saber and tossed it aside. He could not have made this choice before he ignited his weapon. He could not have preplanned it or reasoned it out. Meditation trains us to be here and now, to see things as they are, and to be grounded so our choices aren't made from a place of passion or emotion, but from a place of intuitive insight gained from meditation. The Emperor was hoping to push Luke into acting from a place of hatred, which would have turned him to the dark side. That would have been the wrong choice, and although Luke had been consumed by hatred moments before, he collected himself, regained his stability, and cut off hatred in the present moment.

The actions that we do in the present bear fruit in the future. The teaching on karma becomes more complicated when we consider that karmic fruit can ripen not just in this lifetime, but in the next. But what does this really mean? On the one hand we have emptiness: the human being is empty, made up of five aggregates each of which are themselves empty and constantly changing. There is no permanent, separate self and no soul. On the other hand there is rebirth. It is important to see rebirth as moment-to-moment and forever. Each moment of life is a birth and a death. Joy arises in us and fades away. Perceptions come and go. A skin cell dies and another is reborn. Therefore, despite the fact we have no permanent or separate self we have lived through countless deaths since we first picked up this book. Every moment we are born, and every moment we die, and through it all we continue. Death—the final destruction of our main reactor—is no different.

Imagine a rainbow, perhaps arching over a waterfall outside Theed. We distinguish the rainbow from the waterfall, the sky, and especially from ourselves. However, the rainbow only exists because of the interplay of interdependent conditions: the presence of air, water vapor in the air, sunlight hitting the vapor, and our personal perception and perspective. Each of these factors is impermanent, yet each is necessary for there to be a rainbow. And beyond these conditions and their interplay, there is no unchanging, separate, independent "self" that we can say is by itself the rainbow—and yet rainbows clearly do exist.

But when someone we know dies they are not just different from what they were a moment ago, they are gone. They will no longer come out and have a mock lightsaber duel with us when we knock on their door. But remember the rainbow: a variety of conditions formed it. One of those conditions is sunlight. So what happens to the rainbow when the sun sets and night falls? Does it die? Does it become nothing?

The truth is the rainbow has not become nothing just because we don't see it; it has simply changed. The water vapor that helped give it life has now floated up to form a cloud. The air that held the vapor has moved with the changes in atmospheric pressure created by nightfall to become wind rushing through the hair of Jamillia, the Queen of Naboo—in fact becoming part of her as she breathes it.

The rainbow is no longer there for us to enjoy as a rainbow, and our friend who passed is no longer there for us to enjoy hitting upside the head with the cardboard tubing we pretend is actually Vader's saber. But neither our friend nor the rainbow has become nothing. If we look deeply we will see them again.

Like the rainbow, we too are formations. The five aggregates come together, and through their interplay there is this thing we call the human being. There is no unchanging, separate, independent "self" that is by itself a human being—nonetheless human beings do exist. We are neither an illusion nor permanent and distinct.

Just as the person you are at this moment is an extension of the person you were in the previous moment, the shape you take after the body shuts down is a continuation of who you were at the instant of death. That means our will, desire, craving, feelings, perceptions, and so forth carry on. But what does that mean?

One Buddhist monk puts it this way: "As there is no

permanent, unchanging substance, nothing like a self or soul passes from one moment to the next. So quite obviously, nothing permanent or unchanging can pass or transmigrate from one life to the next. It is a series that continues unbroken, but changes every moment."

The Buddha used a very simple model to reconcile the insight of no-self and rebirth. He took a lit candle and indicated that the flame represented a human being. Then taking another candle he touched the unlit wick against the flame of the first candle. The wick caught fire and there was a flame on the second candle. The flame on the second candle is a continuation of the flame on the first. We cannot say that the second flame is the first because they are clearly on two different candles. At the same time, however, we cannot say that they are wholly different because one directly gave rise to the other. We can take five, ten, a hundred candles and light one off the other. The flame on each would be an extension of the one before it. None the same and none different.

"Similarly," continues the monk quoted above, "a person who dies here and is born elsewhere is neither the same person, nor another. It is the continuity of the same series. The difference between death and birth is only a thought-moment: the last thought-moment of this life conditions the first thought-moment of the so-called next life."

So the question "What exactly is reborn?" is not a proper question, not the kind of question that can be meaningfully answered. Everything is reborn—all matter and energy in the universe are constantly transforming, never being destroyed or created. Buddhism says we can experience a "past life" because we are a continuation of that life. Birth and death are merely ideas—nothing separates us from one moment to the next. But every moment we have the freedom to choose.

Life is just a series of infinitesimally brief moments running together like frames in a strip of film—each moment instantaneously occurs and passes. As one Buddhist said, "If all things did not arise and vanish instantaneously, bad done in the previous instant would not depart. If bad done in the previous instant had not yet departed, good of the next instant could not be realized in the present."

In other words, Vader was able to turn his life around in an instant because the world is arising and passing away, appearing and vanishing moment by moment. The potential to change was always available to him. It was only because of force of habit or because he could not see the error of his ways that he never seized it until that fateful day when a tribe of gamboling teddy bears helped overthrow the mighty Empire. Luke's actions touched something deep within Anakin. His decision to throw away his saber, to choose compassion rather than violence—so different from the decision that Anakin made all those years before— revealed the true, transformative meaning of the Force to Vader. He broke from his karmic prison and snatched the freedom available to him, realizing at last that good had always been there.

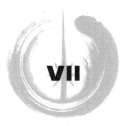

NIRVANA AND THE WAY
OF THE FORCE

"The Force is…an energy field created by all living things. It surrounds us and penetrates us. It binds the galaxy together."

—OBI-WAN KENOBI IN *A NEW HOPE*

Yoda shows us that letting go doesn't need to be a dramatic, painful, or emotional experience. Letting go of concepts doesn't need to be life and death, even when they're about life and death. Yoda has seen entire star systems plummet from peace into chaos. He has witnessed the Sith ascend to galaxy-wide domination and the Jedi crumble into ruin. He knows he has reached the end of his life and that his mortal enemies would mock his final words. Yet he is not attached to a vision of the way things should be. He does not despair his lost Republic, his dead Jedi, or his own failures. He knows twilight is upon him and night will soon fall. Yoda is able to let go because he sees through concepts of life and death. He sees the truth of "the way of things." Seeing and abiding in that truth is the ultimate state of freedom—nirvana.

Luke Skywalker, when he faced Darth Vader in Cloud City while still a novice Jedi who had not yet understood "the way of things," handles things much less gracefully.

"Obi-Wan never told you what happened to your father," Darth Vader intones as Luke scrabbles away from the dark lord.

"He told me enough! He told me you killed him." Luke reaches the end of the Cloud City gantry. There's no escape from what's to come.

"No," Vader says. "I am your father."

"No. No. That's not true! That's impossible!"

"Search your feelings. You know it to be true."

Luke's reaction is a thunderclap of despair. "No! No!"

Luke's denial of the truth of his parentage was a moment of despair. Everything he believed in, the foundation of his faith and moral code, his very identity—they were all shattered by Vader's calculated revelation. Luke responded poorly to despair—he fled from it. Leaping from the gantry, he sought escape in oblivion. For Luke, Vader's words had rendered his existence, even his value for the universe, utterly meaningless. And Luke couldn't bear it.

When we cling to our concepts about life as if they are reality, our world takes a fifty-story swan dive the moment those beliefs are stripped away. Luckily Cloud City still had weather vanes. The one that Luke tumbled upon saved him from death and gave the kid a second chance to gaze deeper into his despair and see nothingness was just another concept that diverted him from the truth.

To be clear, Luke's concepts weren't the trigger for his despair. Neither was the stripping away of them. It was his attachment to concepts, perceptions, and beliefs that caused him to fall to pieces when the truth behind his assumptions was revealed. Buddhist teachers since the Grand Jedi Master himself—the Buddha—have been urging people to let go of their attachments and get to the bottom of reality. When you reach the bottom you aren't left with nothing—you're left with the truth. The truth is nirvana.

Nirvana literally means "cessation." In the time of the Buddha a common metaphor for suffering was the burning of fire. The Buddha would say that everything, body and mind, is burned by the fire of suffering. Nirvana is attained when the fire is put out, when suffering ceases.

The fire of suffering is extinguished when identification with and attachment to desire, views, ideas, and composite phenomena are put to an end. For a fire to burn certain conditions are necessary—heat, fuel, and oxygen. If one of those conditions is removed the fire ceases. Suffering, like a blazing fire, burns because of specific karmic conditions. Among those conditions is attachment. If attachment is removed the fire of suffering is extinguished. With discipline and training, we can calm impulses, wrong views, and other things that result in attachment or aversion to aspects of life. We could say that Yoda's "way of the Force" is a practice of calm reflection, mindfulness, and deep commitment that transforms the dark side path. With calmness and mindfulness—supported by understanding of what Yoda calls "the way of things"—the fire of suffering goes out.

Mindfulness means seeing the world as it is without the veil of ideas or concepts and acting accordingly. When the thought "I" ceases and suffering drops away, that is nirvana. We all have perceptions of ourselves and others. We look at ourselves and say I am charming, timid, or boorish; we look at Darth Vader and say he is wretched and evil. We have a fixed unconscious view of ourselves and others and tend to act based on our belief in that view. Nirvana is the understanding that there is no "I," no real, unchanging self, neither for ourselves or for others. But nirvana is also not the belief that there is not a self. Both views—that there is a real "I" and that there is none—are momentary points of view. Both must be relinquished to attain true peace.

In *The Empire Strikes Back*, Obi-Wan told Luke, "Many of the truths we cling to depend greatly on our own point of view." I have to admit when I first heard these words I took them as a cop out. They seemed like a lame excuse for lying. I thought, "Just own up to your lie, Obi-Wan. Tell Luke your story about Anakin being killed by Darth Vader was a crock of bantha poodoo you fabricated because you didn't think he was ready for the truth." Now I understand that Obi-Wan was pointing to something much more profound, something Buddhists call the Two Truths.

According to Buddhism there are two kinds of truth: relative truth and absolute truth. Relative truth is truth viewed from within the interdependent web of the symbiont circle. From this point of view, we see things only partially. Luke hears Obi-Wan's justification for lying to him and is annoyed. He struggles with the task placed before him and worries about whether he can kill his father. He turns himself in to the Empire and grows angry when the Emperor taunts him. At each moment Luke sees himself as a fixed personality that things happen to. This view isn't entirely wrong. It is the natural way that all beings see the world after all. It's just that it is a limited view.

Absolute truth is grasped when we deeply understand what the symbiont circle implies about reality: when all things are conditioned and dependently produced, nothing can have an unchanging essence, or self, of its own. When Luke gets the absolute truth, he lets go of concepts of self and other and no longer clings to the way things are in the moment as the way they always are and will be. He stops believing he is separate from his father or that he is a fixed person with an identity that can be destroyed by the Emperor. Absolute truth is the reality that Obi-Wan's symbiont circle points to. Luke cannot be separated from the universe. And the universe can't exist without Luke.

In *Attack of the Clones* Obi-Wan tracked Jango Fett—the man behind an assassination attempt on Padmé—to the water world of Kamino. The seas outside Tipoca City on Kamino swelled. On Kamino oceans dominate the surface of the planet and their waves rolled and crashed like the troubled thoughts in Obi-Wan's mind. Each of those waves had a beginning, a middle, and an end. Some waves were bigger than others. Some crested quickly, while others rolled on for several seconds. Some were beautiful and some ugly. Looking out on those waves, Obi-Wan would have been able to contemplate both their relative and their absolute nature.

From the point of view of relative truth, a wave is a wave. It is born, exists for a span of time, and dies. If we look at ourselves from the relative point of view, we may experience a lot of anxiety, because we are caught in a conceptual view of the world that isolates self from other, birth from death, joy from suffering. But from the point of view of absolute truth these concepts aren't real. Like a hologram of a Rancor monster they can't do anything to us (there is no real "us" to do anything to), they're just a vision. From the point of view of the absolute, a wave is ocean. The wave arises out of, abides in, and returns to the ocean, all while being indivisible from it. You cannot separate the wave from ocean. And you can't have the ocean without the wave.

Our lives are like waves and nirvana is like the ocean. When tangled in concepts and ideas about our world, we see "I" and "mine"; we are tossed about by what happens to "us" and "ours." But when we disentangle ourselves from conceptuality, where we previously saw crashing waves of "I" and "mine" we see only the peace of an infinite and all-encompassing sea. If Obi-Wan looked out at the waves on the seas of Kamino with the insights gleaned from understanding the symbiont circle, he'd know the nature of the waves is ocean; he'd understand that each discrete moment of relative experience is but a shimmer on the surface of the absolute. Relative and absolute truth are interconnected. In a way, the absolute truth is understanding what relative truth really is. Joy and suffering arise and fade away together.

We can learn more about nirvana by reflecting on the Force. Recall what Obi-Wan and Yoda said of it in the original trilogy. In *A New Hope*, Obi-Wan Kenobi describes the Force as an energy field created by all living things. "It surrounds us," he explains, "and penetrates us. It binds the galaxy together." Yoda echoes Obi-Wan in *The Empire Strikes Back*: "Life creates [the Force], makes it grow. Its energy surrounds us and binds us. You must feel the Force around you. Here, between you...me...the tree...the rock...everywhere!"

We may imagine the Force as some sort of invisible river of magical energy or an intangible well of mystical power that can be accessed and manipulated. This perception sets up the Force as distinct from us, a tool used by a Jedi or Sith to compel others or to batter foes. But if we look deeper into what Obi-Wan and Yoda say we see that the Force, like nirvana, is not separate from us; it is a part of us—surrounding, penetrating, and binding us with it and the galaxy.

The Force, Obi-Wan tells us, surrounds us. Everywhere we look the Force is present. That means when Luke battles TIE fighters in the darkness of space, the Force is there. When he flounders through the snowdrifts of Hoth, he is with the Force. Yoda says the Force is here and everywhere. No matter where Yoda, Luke, or even Han Solo find themselves—the Force is there. The same is true with nirvana. It's always present, within us and around us.

The Jedi say the Force binds the galaxy together. This is the same as saying all things in the galaxy are interdependent. The air depends on the tree and the tree depends on the air. The two are bound up with each other. This sort of relationship we have been calling interdependence, but it could just as easily be called the Force or nirvana. The reality is that the two—air and tree—are inseparable. However we describe these things, the label does not alter the truth.

Obi-Wan says the Force surrounds us and binds us, and

it also penetrates us. It enters into our body from every direction. Penetrating us it becomes part of us. We know from Qui-Gon that communication with the Force is present in every living cell in the form of midi-chlorians. The midi-chlorians are the source of all life. Qui-Gon told Anakin Skywalker in *The Phantom Menace*, "Without the midi-chlorians life could not exist." In turn, Yoda revealed to Luke the fact that life creates the Force. Put simply, the Force produces the life of midi-chlorians and this life creates the Force. The Force creates life and life creates the Force. This cycle is present in every living cell, in everything—a relationship of interpenetration.

Some speak of becoming one with the Force or entering nirvana. Such ideas are not quite right. A person cannot become something he already is. Based on our interpretation of the Force we know that Luke was already one with the Force long before he began his Jedi training. Luke cannot exist outside of the Force because it penetrates him and he in turn penetrates it. In fact, he and the Force exist in perpetual interpenetration. Likewise, nirvana is not something entered into. Nirvana is not found outside or later—we are nirvana, right here, right now. Looking deeply we see that there is absolutely no distinction between Luke and the Force, nor any between nirvana and us.

Our nature is the nature of nirvana. It is part of us like a Tatooine sand dune is part of Tatooine or a Kamino wave is part of the ocean. The wave may seem to be distinct from the ocean, but both wave and ocean are by nature water. In the same way, we are inimitable and wondrous waves of nirvana forming, breaking, and returning to the source. We are an expression of nirvana—of the world as it is.

Investigating life with mindfulness and effort we can also destroy these barriers that exist only in the mind. Looking deeply we can see that we are part of all of life. Our bodies, thoughts, and consciousness are not distinct from the world; they do not exist independently—our true nature is the nature of the undying nirvana. Death does not reduce us to nothing. We can never become nothing because our nature is emptiness and that means we are made up of everything. The practice of living Force-mindfulness allows us to touch our no-birth, no-death nature and helps us remove the shroud of the dark side and see the truth that life just is, and we can never be outside it. This realization shatters the illusion of death.

Examine the Force with the insight of interdependence. On the surface, it may appear that the Force is divided. There is the good side of the Jedi and the dark side of the Sith. But the two cannot exist independently; they define each other. We need the dark side to know the good side, to know the right choices to make. Looking deeply into the good side of the Force we find the dark side, showing us the path to avoid. In Buddhist terms you cannot have nirvana without samsara. Samsara is the suffering in life. It's the repetitive cycle of craving, attainment, loss, forgetfulness, and sorrow that we are bound up in.

It's common to think that nirvana and samsara are unrelated opposites. One is the cessation of suffering and the other is bondage to suffering. However, like the dual aspects of the Force, nirvana and samsara interpenetrate one another. You can't have nirvana without samsara. You can't have the absolute without the relative. We realize freedom and bondage simultaneously.

You don't run away from the dark side to realize the good side. But, at the same time, you must recognize that the dark side is not the same as the good side. They are interconnected, but not the same. Turning to the dark side, sleepwalking through samsara, is not the same as living a realized life. By facing up to the dark side, by understanding samsara, we gain insight into the good and really know nirvana. But facing up to the dark side doesn't mean giving in to it. You can't become a realized Jedi by practicing the arts of the dark side. Like Yoda told Luke, "If once you start down the dark path, forever will it dominate your destiny."

Our destinies are currently dominated by samsara because we fail to examine it thoroughly and see it for what it is. Because we are attached to the idea of an enduring self, we struggle to acquire what we prefer or to make ourselves into invented images of perfection—enlightened beings, Jedi masters, Republic senators, or roguish space pirates. This samsaric struggle is the path of the dark side. The Sith are caught in the idea of a separate self: "They think inward, only about themselves." The Sith strive to attain more for themselves: power, control, eternal life. Their goal is to empower the self.

The Jedi, on the other (cyborg) hand, are about unlearning blind assumptions, letting go, allowing the Force to guide their actions. They are, as Anakin put it, "selfless." By this he means they aren't out for power for themselves—for an illusory self—or struggling to achieve an ideal state of mind or behavior. The Jedi are concerned with living a realized life, a life of self-discovery. They strive to realize their true nature and express it without pretense. Their true nature, and yours, is nirvana.

If we understand what nirvana is, it's easy to see that Buddhism isn't a quest for nirvana. It's more of an attitude toward life, or a way of being, that allows the truth of nirvana to reveal itself. We needn't isolate ourselves from normal life or try to avoid ordinary tasks (like cleaning droids and repairing junky freighters) in order to attain transcendent states or hokey Jedi powers. We simply continue to do everyday things, but with the "deepest commitment" to doing them mindfully and always with the ready attitude of (re-)discovering the dynamic, immediate truth of their reality.

You don't have to leap from a gantry or ascend to the pinnacle of the Jedi ranks to touch your true nature. You just need to bring your full presence to what you're doing, even if you're just scrubbing muck off your R2 unit.

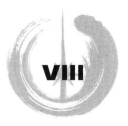

THE EIGHTFOLD PATH THAT TRANSFORMS THE DARK SIDE

"Your focus determines your reality."

—JEDI MASTER QUI-GON JINN
IN *THE PHANTOM MENACE*

Luke is repeatedly warned to beware the dark side. If Luke is not aware of the dark side as it arises within him, he might be swept away by it and suffer his father's fate. The Eightfold Path is the way that helps us maintain our stability so we are not seduced by selfishness, confusion, anger, hatred, and jealousy.

The Buddha was the creator and original master of the Eightfold Path. Wherever the Eightfold Path is practiced, the Buddha taught, joy, peace, and insight are there. Thus, the Eightfold Path does not lead us away from the dark side to peace and insight, but when put into practice, the Path is peace and insight. In other words, the Path is not a means to an end like the Jedi trials; the Path is a reward in itself.

We walk the Path by observing right speech, action,

livelihood, effort, mindfulness, concentration, view, and thought. The eight factors of the Path are grouped into the three categories of moral virtue, meditative cultivation, and wisdom. The perfection of these three aspects of the human being is essential in order to realize nirvana. In the first category, moral virtue, is right speech, right action, and right livelihood.

RIGHT SPEECH

In the Star Wars universe it's a cinch to communicate across the vast expanse of the galaxy. With comlinks, holograms, and astromechs capable of boosting signals, people can get in touch with others light years away in real time. Despite all these technological advances, communication between individuals can sometimes be very difficult.

"I think it is time we informed the Senate that our ability to use the Force has diminished," Mace Windu concluded in *Attack of the Clones.*

To which Yoda replied: "Only the Dark Lords of the Sith know of our weakness. If informed the Senate is, multiply our adversaries will."

Communication had broken down between arms of the government tasked with protecting the lives and welfare of the people. The Jedi could not talk to the Senate, and senators—split into fractions by the coming war—could not talk to each other. Anakin could not fully convey his troubles to Yoda in *Revenge of the Sith* because he was afraid of revealing his relationship with Padmé. Luke and Vader had a hard time really connecting, as they were trapped in viewing each other as nemeses and constantly trying to kill each other.

Right speech is about establishing productive and honest communication that is beneficial to both the speaker and the hearer. The Buddhist precept about using truthful speech is related to observing right speech:

> Aware of the suffering caused by unmindful speech and the inability to listen to others, I am committed to cultivating loving speech and deep listening in order to bring joy and happiness to others and relieve others of their suffering. I will refrain from uttering words that can cause division or discord, or that can cause the family or community to break. I am determined to make all efforts to reconcile and resolve all conflicts, however small.

When Luke approached Vader on the forest moon of Endor, he was practicing right speech, trying to resolve the conflict between himself and his father, and turn the Dark Lord back to the good side.

"I know there is good in you," Luke affirmed. "The Emperor hasn't driven it from you fully."

Luke's words didn't inspire an immediate turnaround in his father, but those truthful and compassionate words laid the groundwork that made Anakin's redemption possible.

Right speech also requires abstention from telling lies, from gossip and discordant words, and from abusive or cruel language. Chancellor Palpatine, the master of the dark side, was also a master of violating right speech. In *Attack of the Clones*, after years of careful manipulation and deception, Palpatine has finally obtained what he sought— emergency powers to rule the Republic like a tyrant. His first words upon receiving this authority are the darkest of lies. With false sincerity he says, "It is with great reluctance that I have agreed to this calling. I love democracy—I love the Republic. The power you give me I will lay down when this crisis has abated." Of course he never intended to relinquish his authority and, instead, goes on to rule through terror and murder for decades.

The failure to speak rightly isn't a "sin," but it is unwise and harmful. The Buddhist view isn't that we will be punished for telling lies and using words that create division— but we do bear the karma of our speech. "All beings are the owners of their deeds, the heirs of their deeds; their deeds are the womb from which they spring. Whatever deeds they do—good or evil—of such they will be the heirs." This is true with all the factors of moral virtue: speech, action, and livelihood. Palpatine's deeds, his lies and deception, do not wait until some imagined afterlife to produce suffering. They bring him suffering in the midst of his rule as Emperor. He can find no joy in the authority he achieved through guile and so he sits in the dark, a shriveled figure, scheming and suffering.

With right speech, words are viewed as a treasure that should only be brought out when they are useful and when the time is right. In *Attack of the Clones*, Padmé uses right speech when she reminds Anakin that his anger is only natural and that it is not his fault that his mother died. Not only were these words true, they were also kind and loving. Right speech requires the use of truthful, loving words intended to inspire self-confidence, joy, and hope in others.

Right speech, in this case, means we learn when to listen deeply and not talk. By listening deeply to others, as Padmé listened to Anakin, we can hear what they are saying and what is being left unsaid. This affords us the opportunity to find the "right" thing to say, the loving and supportive words that lessen the burdens of others.

RIGHT ACTION

One way to investigate our actions is to look at their results, the fruits they produce. If the fruit is putrid and looks like it should be fed to the dianoga in the Death Star trash compactor, then our actions of the past might not have been right action. If the fruit is sweet and brings us and others true joy like shuura, the tasty Naboo fruit Anakin and Padmé enjoyed, then it is likely that the action that produced it was right. Being mindful of the living Force and our bodily actions will allow us to recognize the variety of fruit they produce.

In *Revenge of the Sith*, Anakin broods in the Jedi Council Chamber, torn between doing his duty and saving his wife. To protect the life of the one he loves means abandoning everything he believes in and embracing the enemy he has sworn to defeat. To save Padmé he must turn to the dark side.

It's important not to believe your actions are right just because you gain something (like dark side powers) or experience pleasure from them. Palpatine might have cackled insanely when he finished off Mace, but the "unlimited power" he got through his life of evil action never brought him the satisfaction he craved. Power only leaves the powerful craving more.

To practice right action earnestly it is essential that we investigate the intentions behind our actions. Generosity is right action when it is the act of giving without any expectation of return. Anakin's offer to help the stranded Qui-Gon Jinn and Padmé in *The Phantom Menace* is an example of right action. Giving ourselves in time and material resources to those in need is a true act of compassion and one that is a joy unto itself. But if the intention behind the act is not grounded in compassion, then it can lead to the dark side.

Selfish gains are not a good measure of the quality of an act. Anakin said the Sith think "only about themselves" while the Jedi "care about others." Deeds that bring joy to yourself and others, that ease another's pain, that give someone the shot in the arm they want or the restraint that they need—those are right action worthy of a Jedi.

RIGHT LIVELIHOOD

Our vocation can support our effort to live with the spirit of awakening. It can also undermine our efforts and lead us into confusion. A job that causes damage to others and the world would not be right. It wouldn't be right because it is unwise; the damage we cause would return to us via Obi-Wan's symbiont circle.

One way to see if our job is right livelihood is to compare it to Jabba the Hutt's enterprise. Jabba has his fat, stubby fingers in every one of the pots the Buddhists warn us to avoid. He dealt largely in illegal "spice" trade—an illicit drug in the Star Wars galaxy. He peddled people in the slave trade and served them up to his pet Rancor when they got out of line. Jabba lies, cheats, and steals to maintain his position. He doesn't hesitate to murder and will happily pay you 35,000 credits for a living Wookiee (but you've got to prove you're his kind of scum first).

If we look at any job and find that Jabba would enjoy a strong presence there, we may want to reflect on the direction of that employment and see if it is leading to happiness or suffering.

RIGHT EFFORT

The second category of the Path is the category of meditative cultivation. Meditative cultivation focuses on nurturing heart and mind through right effort, right mindfulness, and right concentration. Right effort is diligent action or thought that leads to spiritual freedom. Right effort means to live one's life with the spirit of awakening, the spirit of finding out "who you are." In *The Empire Strikes Back* Yoda says, "A Jedi must have the deepest commitment, the most serious mind." This kind of determination is part of the practice of right effort, which may also be defined as a balanced commitment to truly recognize and accept ourselves and things as they are right now. "The deepest commitment" and "the most serious mind" are needed to be a Jedi. They are also required for sincere Buddhist practice.

Right effort is not a struggle. Right effort shouldn't be harsh or extreme. It's a balanced practice of ease and care. If our practice is a struggle because we're unable to meet the severe standards we've established for ourselves then we'll abandon it, and that would be unfortunate. Punishing ourselves for failing or for being swept away by our emotions is not helpful. We have to accept the way things are before we can see them clearly and find a path of action. A balance between recognizing our humanity and working to improve things has to be struck.

There is a Buddhist story that illustrates this, about a monk named Sona, who had been a musician. The Buddha pointed out that, with stringed instruments like the lute, if strings are too taught, the instrument is not tuneful and fit for playing—and the same is true if they are too slack. But if the strings are neither too tight nor too slack, a musician can bring forth beautiful, tuneful music. The same is true with Buddhist practice. The deep commitment of a Jedi is necessary, but our intensity should be tempered by a realistic outlook. If it is not, the too-taut string of (overly) serious effort may snap.

There are four functions to right effort. The first is to pacify unwholesome seeds that have already blossomed in our minds. "Unwholesome" means anything that does not correlate with peace, happiness, and freedom. This means, among other things, the dark side energies of fear, anger, and aggression. This function is the opposite of what the Emperor employs to tempt Luke to the dark side in *Return of the Jedi*: "Use your aggressive feelings, boy! Let the hate flow through you."

When hate and aggressive, dark-side feelings have entered our consciousness we can remember to practice as Qui-Gon taught and become aware of the present moment and the state of our mind. Recognizing the presence of the dark side in us, we do not allow it to pull us into actions that we will regret. We practice mindful breathing and allow the emotion to pass, and in this way we stave off the path of suffering.

Letting go of dark side energies is complemented by the second function of right effort: preventing unwholesome seeds from manifesting in the mind in the first place. Although hatred, anger, aggression, and other mental formations of the dark side are unwholesome, if we are practicing the way that transforms the dark side, they can nonetheless be transformed into wholesome elements. If we recognize the dark side when it is present in our mind we can practice Yoda's method of calm reflection and gain insight into our hate and aggression and the things that have helped them arise.

The third function of right effort is to cultivate and raise wholesome seeds in the mind. Wholesome seeds are not ideas about living a chaste, upright life—but rather, they are those things that bring us peace, joy, and freedom on a deeply spiritual level. Living simply, taking time to enjoy life, and appreciating our loved ones are ways one can practice the third function.

Once wholesome seeds have bloomed in our mind consciousness we can turn to the final function of right effort,

namely sustaining the wholesome seeds that we've cultivated. We can keep wholesome seeds strong in our mind
by nourishing them with mindfulness and concentration.
Breathing in and out in mindfulness is an ever present light
of peace that brings ease and contentment.

RIGHT MINDFULNESS
AND CONCENTRATION

Right mindfulness refers to the practice of nonjudgmen-
tal attention that doesn't label or conceptualize. Qui-Gon
instructed Anakin to "watch me and be mindful." Mindfulness is sometimes called "appropriate attention." Buddhist
practice is to find ways to bring appropriate attention to
everything. It's called a practice because our attention usually wanders away from what we are doing in the moment,
and so we must practice bringing it back.

Right concentration is single-pointed action. When
we do something with right concentration the notion of
"self" falls away and we become one with the action. In
The Empire Strikes Back, Yoda screams "Concentrate!" when
Luke wobbles out of a handstand, kicking the ancient Jedi
master to the ground. Luke was troubled by visions; his
concentration was not single-pointed and so his action was
unfocused too. The moment the notion of self intrudes,
concentration wobbles and trouble follows.

Throughout this book we have seen how important
mindfulness and concentration are to the Jedi and to every
Buddhist practice.

RIGHT VIEW

The third type of practice one undertakes on the Path are practices of wisdom. Wisdom is the aspect of ourselves that is developed through profound investigation into life. The two parts of wisdom are right view and right thought.

Right view means seeing things as they are—beyond the conceptual. A Jedi Youngling might be surprised when she sees Mace Windu's purple lightsaber. Jedi sabers are usually blue or green. She might ask, "What color is that?" With right view Mace would say, "It is the color you see." Purple is only a concept.

Right view gives rise to a mind free from the shroud of the dark side. Right view should change the way we look upon the world, as divided and separate, so we see it as it truly is—interdependent and interpenetrated, unified through Obi-Wan's symbiont circle. The dualistic view of self and other, birth and death, Ewok and tree are not right view. Right view is the direct realization of interdependence.

Right view is not belief. When we read about the Four Noble Truths, interdependence, and nirvana, we gain an understanding of them. That intellectual framework helps us move forward. But the understanding that we get from teachings, books, or even the dialogue in a movie is just a conceptual understanding. This type of understanding becomes our ground for insight into things as they truly are. But when we see things as they really are, we no longer see them through the veil of concepts. Right view is actually an absence of views. It is understanding beyond perception, perspective, and belief.

RIGHT THOUGHT

Thought is the forerunner of all action. The second factor of wisdom is right thought. What we think initiates what we do and say. The focus of our thoughts directs our deeds. If one's thoughts are kind and serene, right action will follow—and so will happiness—as surely and as closely as one's shadow.

Right thought is thought that releases dark side energies when they arise in the mind and channels the mind in the direction of the good side of the Force, the place where loving kindness and compassion are dominant. Right thought is the fostering of selflessness and love for all beings in our mind.

In *The Phantom Menace* Obi-Wan Kenobi refers to Jar Jar Binks and Anakin Skywalker as "pathetic life-forms" because they continually get in the way of what Obi-Wan thinks is the best thing to do. This is not right thought. Thinking of other people or things as obstacles in our life creates division and conflict. Right thought does not exclude. It is inclusive—concerned for the well-being of all life-forms.

This does not mean we have to like everyone we come in contact with. But if we are trapped in the idea that they are nothing more than a bother or a representation of what we find contemptible then we are not recognizing their true nature. It is important to keep our hearts open and observe people and phenomena deeply before we pass judgment. We must reflect as Yoda has instructed and ask ourselves, "Am I sure this person is the way I think he is? Am I attached to views and wrong perceptions that are making me narrow-minded and unable to see the truth about this person? Are my opinions rooted in fear and insecurity or prejudice and ignorance?" These types of questions help us to be mindful and to transform the shroud of the dark side.

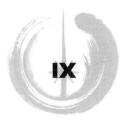

THE WISDOM AND COMPASSION
OF LUKE SKYWALKER

"I am a Jedi, like my father before me."

—LUKE SKYWALKER AND DARTH VADER
IN *RETURN OF THE JEDI*

The Dharma Path, in some ways like the way of the Jedi, is a path of understanding and love. When the Path is walked, these two great qualities of humankind are developed: wisdom (also called understanding) and compassion (also called love).

Wisdom develops from careful observation of our nature and the nature of life. Wisdom is the fruit of meditation (like the calm insight Yoda discussed with Luke), mindfulness (as Qui-Gon and Mace Windu taught), and diligent effort (like the deep commitment and serious mind of a Jedi). Wisdom is the insight of the way things are that frees us from the shroud of the dark side.

But we must cultivate compassion as well. Anakin said compassion "is central to a Jedi's life." The same is true for

Buddhists. Compassion has a special meaning in Buddhism. It's the aspiration and strength to relieve the suffering and sorrow of another.

Unless wisdom and compassion are cultivated equally, imbalance can arise. Perhaps not an imbalance in the Force, but an imbalance in yourself. Compassion developed without wisdom can produce a kind-hearted fool like Jar Jar Binks; while a strong mind developed without compassion can produce a heartless manipulator like Jabba the Hutt.

In Star Wars it is Luke Skywalker in the saga's sixth chapter that best exemplifies the right balance of wisdom and compassion.

After his confrontation with Darth Vader in *The Empire Strikes Back*, Luke knows good still remains in his father. Obi-Wan, however, seems caught by the view that Vader is "more machine than man, twisted and evil." He urges Luke to "confront" Vader and kill him. Obi-Wan apparently fails to recognize that Vader's destiny isn't frozen in carbonite—he can still choose to turn away from evil. Luke believes Vader can make this choice.

Compassion is the intention to relieve someone's suffering, including their delusion, insecurity, and hatred.

In *Return of the Jedi* Luke's wisdom and compassion propel him to turn himself over to the Empire in order to rescue his father. He tells Leia, "There is good in him. I felt it. He won't turn me over to the Emperor. I can save him. I can turn him back to the good side. I have to try." Luke allows himself to be made a prisoner of the Empire in order to "save" Vader, to draw his father out of suffering.

Offering understanding and compassion, Luke appeals to the good Anakin that remained in the shadows of Darth Vader. Reminding him of his life before he turned to evil, Luke says, "You were once Anakin Skywalker, my father." "That name," Vader replies, "no longer has any meaning for me."

"It is the name of your true self," Luke says. "You've only forgotten. I know there is good in you. The Emperor hasn't driven it from you fully." Then Luke directs his father back to himself, to look deeply into his own nature: "Search your feelings, Father... I feel the conflict within you. Let go of your hate"—for it is Vader's hatred, hatred for himself, his failures, among other things, that create the dark side.

It's important we see in this that even Luke Skywalker, with his great mastery of the Jedi ways, of understanding and compassion, cannot with his own power "turn" Vader away from the path of the dark side. This is always the case. We can only offer others compassionate support and wise advice, but only they themselves can remove the shroud of ignorance from their heart and mind. Luke does not tell Vader what he *should* or *should not* do, he simply directs Vader back to himself, to search his own feelings, to investigate his own mind and discover the truth that it is not "too late" for him, that he can still lift himself out of the dark side. This is the Jedi way, and it is also the Dharma way.

In fairness to Obi-Wan, he may have believed encouraging Luke to kill his father was the only way to protect the galaxy from further pain and destruction. Or he could have foreseen how Luke's compassion for his father could turn

Anakin back to the destiny of the chosen one and bring balance to the Force. Obi-Wan actually knew a thing or two about compassion.

In a scene cut from the end of *Revenge of the Sith*, Qui-Gon Jinn returns as an ethereal voice to train Yoda (and later Obi-Wan) to merge with the Force upon death—to become, as Obi-Wan warned Vader, "more powerful than you can possibly imagine." Qui-Gon explains that this ability is achieved "through compassion," with "no thought of self."

Obi-Wan learned this art while he was in his crazy-hermit phase on Tatooine. And he put it to use during his "damn-fool" period in *A New Hope*, when he allowed Vader to cut him down. This power was what Palpatine promised Anakin. It's the power of immortality, but, as Qui-Gon points out, it cannot be achieved through greed or selfishness. The Sith could never learn it.

True compassion, true love never produces suffering. We do not grant it only to those who satisfy our desires, nor reserve it for the happy and prosperous. Real compassion and love are given to everyone, unconditionally. Luke is able to have compassion for his father because he sees how easily he could follow in Anakin's footsteps and succumb to the dark side. Luke recognizes how close he is to a similar fate and sees himself in his father. Luke also has the wisdom to recognize the *source* of his father's evil. That source was not Vader himself, but Vader's ignorance, attachments, misperceptions, self-hate, and his inability to see a way off his karmic path of the dark side.

There is no more compassionate act one person can do for another than offer oneself in order to free another from misery. But even Luke's profound understanding and love falters in the bowels of the Death Star:

Time and time again Luke tries to escape from dueling Vader. He shuts off his lightsaber, he retreats from Vader's attack, and he even hides in order to avoid conflict. However, when Vader threatens Luke's sister, Leia, the young Jedi's composure weakens and in a fury he assaults his father.

Luke charges Vader, besieging him with a flurry of windmill strikes that drive him to the ground. Radiating hate like the white-hot heat of a thousand binary suns, Luke hammers away until his saber slips past his father's defense. *Schink*. Green plasma severs Vader's wrist.

"Good!" cheers the Emperor, gliding in like a vulture sensing blood. "Your hate has made you powerful. Now, fulfill your destiny and take your father's place at my side!"

In this moment, Luke sees that, just like his father, he has become ensnared by hate. Looking at Vader's mechanical stump of an arm, then at his own mechanical, black-gloved hand, Luke realizes he has indeed become like his father. If Luke kills Vader he will not destroy the evil of Anakin Skywalker but only replace it with a new evil—the evil of Luke Skywalker. The failures of Anakin, the weakness of that misguided man, are part of Luke as well. Luke understands the truth that the evil in his father is also in him. It was an evil grounded in misguided intentions, mistaken betrayal, arrogance, ignorance, fear, and self-hate. Realizing this removes Darth Vader's sinister appearance and reveals a sad, pitiable man—a man trapped by his own suffering.

Looking down at his prone father, compassion swells in Luke's heart, and he switches off his lightsaber.

"Never!" he says tossing his weapon aside. "I'll never turn to the dark side."

Luke at this moment does what his father could not do, he transforms suffering. His wisdom parts the shroud of ignorance and shows him that the dark side cannot give him power to "rule the galaxy" or to "save his friends," it can only lead to the misery his father suffered. Recognizing this, his hate disappears, and he says, "I'll never turn to the dark side." Armed now with only wisdom and compassion he does something no weapon can ever do—he defeats the hate in his heart.

Luke's actions show us when you look at the face of evil and hatred, you see fear just below the surface. Luke met his fear on Dagobah and he confronted his hate just moments before. He discarded both along with his saber. Facing the Emperor he declares, "I am a Jedi, like my father before me."

The strength of Luke comes from allowing himself to be vulnerable. He doesn't deny fear, hatred, or suffering. He doesn't allow them to overwhelm him. He meets them with the fearlessness of a true Jedi.

Fear, hatred, and suffering are natural. They're only a problem when we don't have the space within us to allow them to be present. When we do, there's nothing to fear. They come and go—and we see them for what they are. We can't know compassion without suffering. We can't know love without hatred. We may want to destroy Darth Vader but without him we can never be true Jedi. Don't run from your suffering. Don't bludgeon it with mental lightsabers.

Allow it to be, embrace it in compassion—but don't let it consume you. Then you will defeat it as Luke did.

In the Star Wars saga, balance is brought to the Force when Vader defeats the Emperor and removes the plague of the dark side from the galaxy. But the true balance, inner balance, comes earlier: when Vader finally sees the other side of fear and hatred is freedom and love. Anakin may have told Luke that he "saved" him, but it is Anakin's own choice to finally face the dark side within him with courage and honesty that frees him from it. To be in the grips of suffering is to be out of balance, but the practice of meditation brings harmony to the Force and reveals the presence of nirvana. The happiness of this practice is the happiness that is content (but never complacent) to suffer.

While Luke Skywalker best exemplifies the qualities of wisdom and compassion in Star Wars, it is his father, Anakin, who shows us the full range of what it is to be human. Anakin goes from a sweet kid to an arrogant, temperamental young man, to a monster cloaked in the dark side. In his life, he loved people, at times he hated himself, he sought the approval of his teachers, he selflessly tried to help others, he made mistakes, and he committed the most unspeakable crimes. But in the end he finds freedom from the dark side.

Many of us carry the burden of self-hatred. We note our failings, weaknesses, prejudices, and all our other ugly qualities and think, "I am no good; I'm a liar, a fake. I speak harshly to people and think cruel thoughts of my friends and family. I'm a loser and a failure in everything I do." We think the way of wisdom and compassion and the practice of mindfulness are beyond us because there is so much hatred, anger, and fear in our heart. We have become so trapped in the darkness of our own suffering and delusion that we fail to see the light of peace, joy, and freedom available to us right now.

Yet the lesson of Anakin's experience teaches us that everyone, even the most wicked, has the seed of liberation in his heart. That seed is waiting for us to help it grow. We can help it grow right now by learning to *stop*. Literally stop what you're doing and find your breath. Stay with your breath and allow the poisonous stream of negative thinking that judges you and demands perfection to prattle away. You are right where you need to be. You are home. Your self-loathing and destructive thinking are just habits. Thoughts are no more real than nightmares. At this moment you are perfectly complete. Take time each day to stop and you'll discover that freedom is always available. This freedom is your birthright.

If Darth Vader can find freedom then each of us can too.

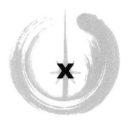

MAKE FRIENDS WITH JAR JAR

"Hello, boyos!"

—JAR JAR BINKS, *THE PHANTOM MENACE*

The Jedi practice meditation. Luke's training under Yoda on Dagobah is a form of meditative concentration—albeit one practiced while upside-down! Qui-Gon observes and calms his fears and aggressive feelings with meditation. Anakin meditates on the growing dread and anxiety he feels over his mother's plight. And Yoda meditates to investigate the dark side and the mysteries of life. Even Vader had a dedicated meditation chamber aboard the Executor, his arrowhead-shaped Super Star Destroyer.

Despite a common misconception, meditation is not meant to cut us off from the world or to avoid life. Meditation is a practice that helps us experience life fully—to get in touch with reality as it truly is. If a Jedi were to meditate in the way taught by the Buddha he would be meeting life directly, he would not run from himself or find things to distract him. He would sit, breathe, and observe his mind with equanimity and compassion. And from this process the freedom that is understanding develops.

Meditation is the practice of focusing the mind so we become aware of its conditions in the present moment. We observe feelings, thoughts, memories, and desires as impermanent. Even the idea of self—the belief "I am this little green body" or "I am a Jedi master"—is recognized as transitory. We observe feelings and thoughts, but we do not grasp them, and so they fade away. In time meditation brings us to understand, not just intellectually but in our heart, directly, that whatever is of the nature to arise is of the nature to cease. Deep understanding of this frees us from attachment to desperate thoughts like, "I must marry her," or "I must destroy the Jedi Order," or "What's wrong with me? I should be happy!"

Luke enters the dark side cave on Dagobah in order to confront himself, to face his suffering. This is precisely what meditation is. It is the conscious act of calmly taking a look around the depths of our own mind. There are a lot of frightening and ugly things in there, a lot of dark-side elements, but we are careful not to attach to them. We recognize and examine them, calmly, as Yoda instructs Luke to do. This is why it's absolutely essential to find a Buddhist teacher or a dedicated group of meditators to practice with. Without guidance we may lose ourselves in fears or become caught in destructive ideas about ourselves and the world, which can cause serious damage. With proper guidance, we learn not to reject or ignore those elements of ourselves we find frightening. We discover that they are complexes, fears, desires, and misunderstandings that are both deep and shallow. But by observing them we realize they are all impermanent, they are all just ideas, and we slowly remove layer after layer of the dark side shroud.

It is important to develop understanding of the impermanent nature of things. One way to do this is by observing our feelings. Feelings can be pleasant, neutral, or unpleasant. A pleasant feeling could be the excitement and anticipation we feel when the words "A long time ago in a galaxy far, far away…" appear on the screen. A neutral feeling could be sleepiness on the third night of camping out for the midnight showing of *Revenge of the Sith*. An unpleasant feeling could be listening to Jar Jar Binks talk.

Pleasant feelings arise in one context, and unpleasant manifest in another. External phenomena and our perceptions of them have an impact on the sensations and thoughts we experience. As phenomena and perceptions shift, feelings alter as well. Observing our feelings we discover that they are not solely "ours." Feelings are formations that are produced by a variety of components. Misperceptions, habits, biology, the food we eat, and objects of perception all impact the way we feel. With meditation we realize that the feeling we experience is just a feeling and not my feeling. This practice helps cultivate equanimity in us—a quality highly regarded among the Jedi!

In *The Phantom Menace*, as Obi-Wan Kenobi hangs desperately just below the rim of the Theed melting pit, he could have easily been lost in his despair. His master lies dying a few feet away, and with Darth Maul poised to strike, his own life seems finished as well. But Obi-Wan steadies himself. Breathing calmly he lets his fear and worry float past him, he remains composed in the face of incredible strain—and he defeats Darth Maul. Later he is confirmed a Jedi Knight for his actions and, presumably, for his display of equanimity.

Equanimity means remaining centered in the midst of life regardless of the intensity of the experience. When a pleasant or unpleasant feeling arises we notice it. We may appreciate a pleasant feeling (like the warm feelings romantic love gives rise to in Anakin), but our appreciation should not go so far as to become attachment. Calmly letting go of a pleasant feeling as it fades is being equanimous. The same is true with unpleasant feelings like anger and hatred. As anger and hatred manifest in us we can use Obi-Wan as a model and follow our breath, remaining centered so our emotions do not carry us away.

Powerful feelings—like anger and hatred—can overwhelm us as they do Anakin at the Tusken camp. That is why Yoda and Obi-Wan Kenobi warn Luke in *The Empire Strikes Back* to beware of anger and not to give in to hate. Those feelings lead to the dark side.

Meditating on our feelings helps us better understand ourselves. Contemplating the mind and the activities of the mind can also deepen self-awareness. In meditation we observe the thoughts, desires, and moods of the mind. Sometimes it is as calm as still water, and other times it is as raucous as the crowd at the Boonta Eve race. But outside of meditation, when our mindfulness is weak, the mind typically functions like Jar Jar Binks. Jar Jar's attention is noticeably unfocused on what he is doing. He fumbles with a tool and gets shocked in the process, his thoughts drift away from his bodily movements and he steps in something foul, he is mesmerized by his visual appetite and confuses conversation. Jar Jar's unmindfulness causes him and others (and us too when we see him on screen!) a great deal of grief. His unmindfulness leads to banishment from his home, ostracizes him from others, and—on several occasions—nearly gets him killed.

Our minds too have "Jar Jar nature." When Jar Jar nature is in full possession of us we do things unskillfully and we bring discomfort to ourselves and to others. We can "transform the Jar Jar within" by practicing mindful breathing, bringing our awareness to the present, scattered state of our mind. Awareness of Jar Jar nature does not mean we try to make our mind shut up or lock it away in some room like Obi-Wan does to the real Jar Jar in *The Phantom Menace* (well, the CG one, at least). We just observe our hyperactive mind and allow it to be that way for as long as it needs to be. If we continue to breath mindfully, without self-judgment or expectation, the Jar Jar within will calm down (but, as we will see below, that's not necessarily the goal of meditation). Sometimes, when the mind is particularly overrun by our galactically restless Gungan nature, we might find it difficult to keep our attention on the breath. That is why it is sometimes good to move our attention away from the head, away from our thinking, and focus it down in the abdomen. We take our mindful breathing low, noticing the rise and fall of the abdomen with each breath.

We can learn from the Jedi in this. Dueling the Dark Lord of the Sith, Darth Maul, in *The Phantom Menace*, Qui-Gon Jinn finds himself in a narrow corridor. His mind is focused on destroying Maul when suddenly the corridor's laser gates slam shut separating him from his opponent. Sensing his opportunity to end the Sith Lord momentarily gone, the Jedi master does not become distracted by lost opportunities nor does he grow anxious about the future. Qui-Gon drops low to his knees, shuts his eyes, and focuses his attention on his breath. Qui-Gon does not flee the moment; he does not attempt to mentally escape the grim peril across from him; he merely takes his breathing low, observing his mind and body.

Qui-Gon's practice helps us keep from being swept away by our thinking, our worrying, and our anxiety. If we are caught up in our thinking we cannot be in direct contact with life. As Qui-Gon tells Anakin, "Remember, concentrate on the moment. Feel, don't think." Of course, we don't just *shut out* our thoughts, but with mindfulness we become aware of them, watch them, and this means we are no longer outright controlled by them.

We have seen Qui-Gon's method of meditation in action. Now let's look more closely at the mechanics of meditation so we can practice it too.

To meditate, find a position in which you can comfortably hold your back erect. Keeping the back straight will help you to be attentive and keep a balanced posture—a direct influence on establishing a balanced mind. A balanced, upright posture will also help you breathe more comfortably and naturally. Aside from holding the back erect, the rest of the position isn't anything to get hung up about. You can sit cross-legged like Master Yoda, kneel like Qui-Gon, or even stand in imitation of Anakin Skywalker. If you prefer a chair (and don't worry that Darth Vader seemed to like this position), that is an equally fine option as well. The aim is to sit in a stable and comfortable position, without getting so comfortable that you fall asleep. A little bit of discomfort is okay; a lot of pain means something's wrong. If you feel pain in your knees or back, readjust your position or you might blow out a knee or slip a disc. Star Wars has plenty of cyborgs; we don't need any more in our world.

As you sit in meditation you can bring your attention to your body. You may notice that your jaw is clenched or your shoulders are tense. We carry a lot of stress in those areas of the body. So we scan our body from the top of our bald, wrinkly head, down to our pointy, green ears and all they way to our bare, clawed feet, relaxing any muscles that are tensed.

With the inhalation, know you are breathing in. With the exhalation, know you are breathing out. Do this by focusing on the natural process of breathing. Do not try to induce a trance or escape into another state of consciousness—just breathe and observe mind and body. There is no place you need to go, no star system or Jedi status that you can attain that could be better or offer more of life than what is here in this moment—so just be aware of it.

If during meditation you find that your thoughts are no longer on your breath but reliving past lightsaber duels or trying to unravel the mystery of Anakin's origins, you will want to diligently—and without judging yourself harshly!—bring your attention back to your breath. Do not become angry if your mind has drifted off to a galaxy far, far away—just return your awareness to the breath. Meditation is not a challenge to be overcome; it is a gift to be enjoyed—the gift of the present moment.

When Jar Jar pops up and shouts, "Mesa back!" just follow your breath (and give the poor guy a smile). Allow him to be, but don't follow him into a wacky adventure. Just stay centered, following your breath. There's no place you need to go, no star system or Jedi status that you can attain that could be better or offer more of life than what's here at this moment—this is all you got; don't shun it.

In the beginning you may find it difficult to keep your mind in contact with the rhythm of your breath. That is natural—your own "Jar Jar nature"—that fidgety, erratic, spastic quality—is the nature of our mind, and it does not want to pay attention to something so boring as our breath. So we may want to look for ways to help keep our attention from bouncing off the walls and, instead, directed on our breath.

One helpful technique is silently counting our breaths. For each cycle of inhalation and exhalation count one. *In... out,* "one." *In...out,* "two." *In...out,* "three." All the way to ten, and then back down to one again. It doesn't matter if you get to ten—it doesn't even matter if you get to three! If you lose count or your mind drifts away, just resume counting from one. Do not become discouraged if it is difficult to remain focused. Mindfulness is a part of each and every one of us; the more we practice, the stronger our mindfulness will become—it just takes time and Jedi-style commitment.

Besides sitting meditation there is another type of meditative practice that we can employ: walking meditation. Walking meditation uses the same principles as sitting meditation, just with the added dimension of movement. We don't see Jedi practicing walking meditation in the Star Wars saga, but we can imagine them strolling carefully and mindfully through the Jedi Temple and along starship corridors. There is a nobility to their walk and a grace that suggests a calm, even mind.

Walking meditation is a very good way for us to practice unifying mind, breath, and bodily action. It begins with taking one step as you breathe in and another step as you breathe out. Your steps are the same as always. You do not exaggerate the movement or walk stiffly. You simply walk as you usually do, but now you are able to enjoy and appreciate your steps in mindfulness. You can do this practice anywhere, anytime. However, when you are in the markets of Mos Espa, attending a session of the Galactic Senate, or running late for a class with Master Yoda you may want to increase the pace of your walk. You may take three or four steps for each inhalation and exhalation. The number of steps depends on your own individual rhythm—I imagine Master Even Piell takes more steps in a breath than a larger Jedi like Master Yarael Poof. It does not matter whether you take two or six steps, or whether you stand 1.2 meters or 2.6, just as long as you remain mindful of your walking.

Many people come to meditation hoping to gain a new-found sense of calm. They settle into a cushion or chair and close their eyes—eager for the enlightenment to begin. That's about the time your inner Jar Jar Binks stumbles into your mind.

"Hello, boyos," he announces, staring around like a crazed sheep.

Not now Jar Jar. Shut up and leave me alone.

But he doesn't go away. He just stands there flapping his gangly arms and jabbering about "mesa" this and "bombad" that. His grin is so vacant you want to scream.

You prefer peace, but all you get is noisy goofballery.

Meditation can't save us from Jar Jar or anything else we don't like. Meditation simply puts us face to face with things as they are right now. And that's right where we're supposed to be.

You may not prefer Jar Jar Binks. You may even hate him. Or there may be times when his particular personality characteristics are not appropriate to the situation (like when you're trying to achieve that coolness exhibited by the wisest Jedi). But when Jar Jar is present—whether in your mind or in real life—the best thing to do is accept his presence, even welcome it. If you try to deny the way things are right now and make them the way you'd prefer them to be, you'll never experience the peace you want.

Jar Jar represents those aspects of ourselves that we don't like. He is the spaziness we feel when we want to be calm. He is the childish buffoonery we experience when we wish we could exude dignity. He is the fumbling fool who gets his mouth caught in energy binders and blunders into a big pile of eopie dung. When we behave like Jar Jar, we want to run away from ourselves and disappear into the Gungan's hidden city. But the truth is that Jar Jar is not really a problem.

Meditation gives us a great opportunity to see firsthand the impermanent nature of our feelings. As we sit, we feel excited, bored, fidgety, doubtful, itchy, impatient, and so on. None of these things match up with the feelings we were hoping to feel. We wonder: Where's the calm? Where's the Jedi serenity? Why the hell does my mind keep leaping around like Jar Jar on fast forward? What am I doing wrong?

It's only natural to ask these questions. It's common to wonder if something is amiss. When your mind is unsettled—during meditation or otherwise—it's not because you're doing something wrong. It's unsettled because it's unsettled. It's not a problem. The real problem is the belief that our minds are supposed to be different than they are at any given moment.

Jar Jar isn't a problem. He's just the way he is. If you need your inner Jar Jar to disappear in order to be calm or even content, then you'll never truly know those things. We don't need to get rid of Jar Jar to be truly calm; we just need to be able to be calm in the presence of Jar Jar. We must accept things as they are in the moment and allow them to be. Don't allow yourself to be swept away by your Jar Jar nature or unbeneficial mental states. Don't be tempted by the dark side. Don't let it move you.

Buddhist meditation shuts its eyes to nothing, excludes nothing, runs from nothing. This can be terrifying at times, but it's the only way to true peace—not just the idea of it.

In meditation, accept everything about yourself. Welcome everything. You want peace? *Make friends with Jar Jar*. And when it's time for him to bump and squirm to the next star system—just let him go. Like all that is impermanent, he'll fade into the background.

Through meditation you see everything is impermanent. Thoughts appear and disappear. Feelings rise and fall. Even those elements of experience we identify as ourselves—our preferences and personalities—come and go. Like the dreams Obi-Wan talked about in *Attack of the Clones*, they "pass in time," only to return again later.

Through meditation we touch the deep calm of no-self, where personality and preferences fall away. Returning to the metaphor of the ocean and the wave, we can say the deep calm of no-self is like the stillness at the bottom of the sea. Our preferences and personalities are like waves atop the wind-tossed sea. As we experience the rise and fall of feelings, thoughts, self, personality, and preferences, the deep calm is always there just below the surface. We can't extract the wave from the ocean or the ocean from the wave; we can't remove self from no-self—the two are interconnected. The goal is not to leave one behind to attain the other. We couldn't even do that if we tried. The point is to see the situation clearly so we can totally live our lives as they are right now.

We don't need to destroy Jar Jar when we see him in ourselves. Personality and preferences are only a problem when we mistake them for a real, permanent self. No-self is only a problem when we mistake it for something other than what we already are. We realize the truth and touch deep calm through the everyday ordinariness of our lives. So make friends with Jar Jar: go to work, pay your bills, be a goofball. "Be at peace with the oneness of things," as one great teacher said; to which another added, "that is the way of things…the way of the Force."

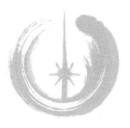

THE PADAWAN HANDBOOK:
ZEN PARABLES FOR
THE WOULD-BE JEDI

PARABLES ON WORTHY CONDUCT

O Apprentice, the way of mindfulness is a difficult one. Commit yourself completely. Always remain diligent because the path of practice is narrow and continuously assailed by the energies of the dark side.

Who is better protected: a Jedi with a legion of his fellow Knights at his side, surrounded by a squadron of battle tanks and ground assault vehicles, or one who conducts himself with honesty and kindness, whose behavior is upright, and whose thoughts are lovingly directed toward all beings? Clearly, one who conducts himself with honesty and kindness, whose behavior is upright, and whose thoughts are lovingly directed toward all beings is better protected because he has guarded himself against the internal armies of the dark side that assail his mind.

Apprentice, it is best not to speak, to tell others how they should live; let your life be your teaching.

Self-pride is a complex that eats the heart and mind of all, including the Jedi. If you think you are greater than other beings, equal to other beings, or less than other beings you have succumbed to self-pride. Guard against these three complexes night and day.

The greatest of all Jedi are not the ones who defeat a thousand opponents; they are the ones who triumph over themselves. Without patience one cannot truly call himself a student of the Way. Develop your patience—make impulse and whim as uncommon to you as honesty and morality are to a Hutt.

Do not abandon the Sith. Do not close your eyes to the Night Sisters. Commit yourself to finding ways to be with those who are gripped by the dark side, so that you can understand their situation deeply and help relieve them of their anguish.

Be an inspiration to your fellow Jedi. Carry yourself with grace and kindness. Do not allow arrogance to distinguish you like fools in martial attire, draped with emblems and medals. A Jedi should wear the simple cloak of his order with humility. When those who avoid the Way, pursuing only what is pleasant, attached to the senses, see one conducted so, they will experience their loss and lament their ways.

Young pupil, always remember:

    Where there is anger, offer kindness.

    Where there is selfishness, offer generosity.

    Where there is despair, offer hope.

    Where there are lies, offer truth.

    Where there is injury, offer forgiveness.

    Where there is sorrow, offer joy.

    Where there is hatred, offer love.

    Where there is evil, offer goodness.

PARABLES ON ATTACHMENT AND DESIRE

Beware of the binding tractor-beam of attachment. For beings attached to their bodies, thoughts, feelings, beliefs, perceptions, or consciousness are imprisoned and can never know true freedom.

To commit to the Way is to give up selfish desires and to live for the benefit of all beings, Gungans, Jedi, and Sith.

Jedi, the joy that arises with bodily pleasure offers fleeting benefits and little sweetness. It is fruit that quickly becomes bitter and over time poisons the one who eats it. The joy that arises with equanimity, that is free from attachment to sensual desires, is sweet and nourishing. Its benefits are profound and ever present. Look carefully, young one, at the objects you desire. Are they truly what you believe them to be? What resides in them that does not reside everywhere?

What do they hold that cannot be found in every element of the galaxy?

Ambition and desire lead to the dark side. Be wise, my determined apprentice, there is no happiness like the happiness of having few desires.

PARABLES ON COMPASSION

A Jedi who is worthy keeps compassion foremost in his thoughts. His compassion extends to all beings in the galaxy. With an open and loving heart he directs these thoughts for their universal benefit:

> May terrestrial beings, arboreal beings, beings of the skies, beings of the seas and oceans, beings of the stars and asteroids, beings visible and invisible, beings living and yet to live, all dwell in a state of bliss, free from injury and sorrow, tranquil and contented. May no one harm another, deceive another, oppress another, or put another in danger. May all beings love and protect each other just as a master loves and protects his Padawan. May boundless love pervade the entire galaxy.

PARABLES ON IMPERMANENCE

The eyes are the tools of deception that conjure the illusion of death. Look! See! There is no death, young one, except that which exists in the mind shrouded by the dark side.

Remember, young Jedi: death lurks around every corner, and it cannot be bargained with. Knowing this, if you are wise, you will put aside all quarrels.

Life is precious to all beings. All beings fear death. Knowing this, my young apprentice, and caring for others as you care for yourself, do not be eager to deal out death.

The Sith cannot escape death. Death, not just of the corporeal body, but of all manifestations of the mind, is inevitable. It is the way of all things, the way of the Force.

When someone is dying of thirst it is too late to dig a well. If you wait until you are upon your deathbed to practice the Way it will be too late. Death will not wait a moment longer than it is ready. Do not be lazy, Padawan; be steadfast as Master Windu.

Life is impermanence. All things are subject to change, and nothing can last forever. Look at your hand, young one, and ask yourself, "Whose hand is this?" Can your hand correctly be called "yours"? Or is it the hand of your mother, the hand of your father? The hand of a senator, the hand of a Jedi? Reflect on the impermanent nature of your hand, the hand with which you once battled a Nexu on Geonosis.

PARABLES ON THE DARK SIDE

A Jedi who is ruled by anger, by hatred, by jealousy, by desire is bound to the dark side just as a mynock binds itself to power cables.

A Jedi who harbors resentment and holds on to the thought "That person was cruel to me and showed me no respect" nourishes the dark side in himself. A Jedi who lets go of resentment and releases pride uproots hatred from himself.

Ignorance is the path to the dark side. One who is practicing the Way must always keep the mind open. Such a one must observe, listen, and learn. The Truth is found in the most unlikely of places.

Like biker-scouts at the head of an army, thought is the vanguard of all action. If your thoughts are influenced by the dark side, your actions will be evil. Observe your thoughts carefully, for they may be leading you down the path of the dark side.

Anger is a powerful emotion of the dark side. It can destroy harmony and lead to argument, conflict, and even death.

When anger arises in you do not give in to it. Remain mindful, observing the anger, but not acting upon it. If you believe someone else is the cause of your anger, look again. They are a mirror reflecting your own mind.

Hatred cannot defeat hatred, young Jedi. If hatred is directed toward you, combat it with kindness. That is the only way to defeat hatred.

PARABLES ON WISE ACTION

Before you act, young one, you must reflect. Reflect unwisely and troubles follow as surely as a droid follows the mandates of his programming. Reflect wisely and troubles are like a shadow in the void of space, unseen and unfelt.

When putting on your robes, igniting your lightsaber, or using the Jedi Mind Trick—when acting in any way— always ask yourself: "Does this action support my true happiness and the true happiness of others? Does this action support my aspiration to transform the energies of the dark side within me?" If so, then you may be sure your action is worthy of the Way.

Thoughts are like tractor-beams that pull you off course. When you act, act! There is no room for thought.

O Apprentice, you inherit the results of your actions in

body, speech, and mind. The ground you stand on today was produced by your actions of yesterday. Actions of worthy conduct produce a stable foundation as firm as permacreate. Unworthy actions produce an unstable path sure to slope into a sarlaac.

PARABLES ON THE MIND

Hold the mind like a cup of water in the hand—still and calm. Like the Force, let thoughts flow through you. Close your hand and you lose yourself.

If you are not aware of your mind, young one, you cannot know it. If you do not know your mind, you cannot care for it. If do not care for your mind, you cannot nourish it and grow in wisdom.

O Learner, you must tame the mind like a handler tames a reek. As an untamed reek can bite and gore so too can the untamed mind destroy you.

The blade of a lightsaber is only as good as its crystal. If the crystal is impure, poorly cut, and fractured, the blade will be dangerous and poor. If, on the other hand, the crystal is pure, well cut, and not fractured, the blade is safe and good. The same is true with the mind. If the mind is impure, poorly trained, and unfocused, the resultant life will be dangerous and poor. But a pure mind, well trained and focused, will bring about a life that is both safe and good.

O Apprentice, you must recognize and abandon the impurities of your mind, the impurities of anger, hatred, aggression, fear, despair, avarice, superfluous desire, obstinacy, arrogance, and jealousy. When you are able to abandon the afflictions of the mind, you will find serenity and happiness.

PARABLES ON MINDFULNESS

Whether sitting, standing, walking, or lying down, be mindful day and night of your bodily position and actions. Whether pleasant, neutral, or unpleasant, be mindful day and night of your feelings. Whether kind, impartial, or cruel, be mindful day and night of your thoughts. Whether focused, ambivalent, or dispersed, be mindful day and night of your state of mind.

Dwelling in meditation, the mind is at peace—emotions rise like a hungry Gooba fish; left alone they cannot disturb the surface.

Harmony arises when there is balance. Balance arises when there is equanimity. Equanimity is the fruit of mindfulness and patience. Take your time, young one, perform every action with complete awareness, and harmony will be your reward.

Attention to the moment reveals what is hidden. With mindfulness of the living Force it is possible to know what is unknown. Focus on what you are doing. Concentration should be fully directed on the object of your inquiry, the object of your task, like the beam of an ion cannon is focused on its target.

A Youngling found a holocron and spoke to a distant master. "I've heard the Way is a doctrine of awakening," the fledgling Jedi said. "What is your method?"

Through the holocron, the master replied, "We walk, we eat, we wash, we sit…"

"What kind of method is that? Everyone walks, eats, washes, and sits."

"Child, when we walk we are aware we are walking. When we eat we are aware we are eating. When others walk, eat, wash, or sit down, they are generally not aware of what they are doing."

PARABLES ON TIME

Always in motion the future is; it is unborn, unsubstantial. It is merely an image, like a hologram of a living being. We can no more touch and feel the future than we can touch and feel a hologram. The future, then, is unreal because it is not present. Only the present is real; only this moment is alive.

When considering the past or the future, dear Apprentice, be mindful of the present. If, while considering the past, you identify with the past, become caught in the past, and burdened by the past, then you have abandoned reality as

Count Dooku abandoned his brethren. If, while considering the future, you identify with the future, become caught in the future, and are burdened by the future, are then you have chased illusions as the Sith chase their dream of immortality. Conversely, when considering the past, if you do not identify with the past, or become caught or burdened by the past, then you, like a once-careless Jedi finding your misplaced lightsaber, have not lost yourself in the past. And if, when considering the future, you do not identify with the future, or become caught or burdened by the future, then, like a Jedi turning away from the dark side, you have not lost yourself in the future.

PARABLES ON WISDOM

The true weapon is the lightsaber of wisdom, which cuts the bonds of ignorance from our mind.

A Jedi ought to choose his words carefully and intelligently. A single word of wisdom says more than a thousand words spoken idly. Thoroughly listen and reflect. The words you utter can have a profound impact on the listener. Will they bring peace or will they cause harm?

I heard these words of a Jedi master one time: Wisdom exists when you understand something and recognize that you understand it and when you do not understand something and you recognize that you do not understand it.

Padawan, do not cling to views or bind yourself to ideology. The knowledge you now have is not changeless, absolute truth. Truth is found in life and is continuously learned and relearned. Be open to the experiences and insights of others; do not remain fixed to a single point of view. The Way of the Jedi is to put aside dogma and touch the truth present here and now in the living Force.

Release all holds on doctrine or dogma, even Jedi ones, and you will be counted among the wise.

AFTERWORD: JEDI VIOLENCE AND NONVIOLENCE

"We are keepers of the peace, not soldiers."
—MACE WINDU IN *ATTACK OF THE CLONES*

As **a person** looking at Star Wars from a Buddhist perspective, I would be remiss were I not to address the issue of violence in those movies. The Buddha's teachings are explicitly nonviolent. Killing and maiming leads very clearly, in the Buddhist view, to suffering in the one killed or injured, in her family and friends, and also in the attacker. Acts of violence can be motivated by anger, hatred, ambition, and jealousy—all factors of the dark side. But can they ever be motivated by compassion? The traditional Buddhist answer is an unequivocal "No," and I don't recommend anyone pursue any path of violence—yet I think there is something important to be learned about ourselves and the nature of violence by looking at the way violence is used by the Jedi Knights.

Can we accept the venerable Jedi, the so-called "guardians of peace and justice," as wise and compassionate people when they use their powers to destroy individuals seduced by greed, hatred, and anger? If their acts of violence are grounded in aggressive feelings and revenge can we say the Jedi are balanced and clear on their view of Obi-Wan's symbiont circle? Let's look at a few specific examples from the Star Wars series.

In *The Phantom Menace*, Darth Maul kills Qui-Gon Jinn out of hatred and ambition: hatred for all things Jedi and ambition to help his master rule the galaxy. Qui-Gon Jinn's murder may have sparked hatred in the heart of Obi-Wan Kenobi, causing the Jedi apprentice to follow in the footsteps of the Sith apprentice. Obi-Wan's scream, "Nooooo!" for example, seems more enraged than anguished, as his face hardens into an assassin's mask. It's the energy of that rage that he apparently used to engage Maul in a lethal dance of plasma and power. Maul was acting out of hatred, and Obi-Wan seemed to retaliate in kind. If this is true, if the young Jedi is motivated by anger, aggression, or hatred, then there is very little difference between the "evil" Darth Maul and the "good" Obi-Wan Kenobi. The dark side of hatred was strong in both.

Before Obi-Wan destroys Maul he has a moment to gather himself and reflect. He hangs, weaponless, above a long shaft leading to certain death (or not so certain if *The Clone Wars* has anything to say about it). During this time Obi-Wan doesn't appear as irate as he'd been before. The mad fire seems to have left his eyes and the hateful rictus is gone from his lips. He draws upon his powers to hurl himself in front of Maul as he ignites his master's saber and slices the Sith Lord in two. The question is: When he actually killed Maul was there hatred in his heart or did those few seconds of reprieve allow him to recognize Maul's sickness and strike him down with sympathy? Did he kill out of some sort of desperate act of compassion to save his dying master? Did he kill to protect the galaxy from the destructive evil of the Sith? I don't know, but if Obi-Wan killed out of hatred than he may as well don the black cloak and take up the red lightsaber of his fallen foe.

Obi-Wan may have believed that because he is a Jedi he is on the "right" to destroy Maul, that the ideals he fights for should be achieved regardless of the means employed. He may rationalize that killing Maul is not only necessary but somehow preferable.

Similarly, in our own world, we may believe that school shooters and terrorists, for instance, should be destroyed at all costs, but we may fail to see the ways in which our lives, culture, and beliefs have helped create them. This is not to say that a person who commits deplorable acts of violence and murder should be pardoned. Of course they shouldn't! We need to do all we can to stop violence when it's happening and prevent it from propagating into the future. But to fail to recognize our contribution—however small it might be—to the evil in the world, to say evil exists *only* in the Other, is the way we create more evil and suffering.

Simply thinking we can kill "evil-doers" and in so doing end evil is naïve. We must together confront the evil in humanity's heart, and engage people's minds with compassion and love and thereby help them out of the poverty, social injustice, and ignorance that is the cause of their dissatisfaction and hostility. We do not need to wait until they attack to help remedy our differences. We can act with considered goodwill now before there is more violence. This is a difficult course of action and much harder than wiping them out with satellite-guided bombs or Death Star–like weapons, but it is the only way we can stop the cycle of violence.

Love is not passive, it is active. Love is not weak, it is courageous. Love means standing up to those who are harming us and others, and stopping them. We stop them with firm hands, but compassionate hearts. When terrorists bring violence to our shores we must respond calmly and not allow anger or fear to overwhelm us. We can respond with compassion in our hearts. We can respond with fearlessness and nonviolent resolve to bring peace and justice to the world. We can look deeply and see that communities that support violence are often acting out of fear and the delusion that they are under attack. They may have misperceptions about us and may see us as the terrorists. They may even say the terrorists are right to attack us and we are wrong to attack them.

Right or wrong violence does not stop unless we set aside the view that "they" are evil and "we" are separate from them. If we find ways to talk with our adversaries so that we may understand their suffering and allow them to understand ours, so that we may make evident our "symbiotic link," we may put an end to the cycle of violence.

In *Attack of the Clones*, Obi-Wan and Anakin Skywalker are in pursuit of Count Dooku, the supposed mastermind of a galactic war. Obi-Wan tells Anakin it's important that they catch Dooku so they "can end [the] war right now." The intention behind their thoughts of killing Dooku is admirable. They hope to prevent an escalation of the Clone War and avert further loss of life—both acts of compassion. But their compassion does not appear to extend to Dooku himself. When they finally confront him, Anakin's anger is evident. He tells Dooku that he must pay for all the Jedi he killed that day. Thus Anakin is not motivated by compassion but by revenge.

When Anakin charges Dooku, attempting to take the Sith Lord on alone, his attack is reckless and unfocused. At that moment Anakin was in the grips of the dark side, swept away by anger and hatred. There's no room for wisdom or compassion when you're pissed, only the all-consuming demand for payback.

In attempting to discover whether the violent acts committed by Jedi can be described as being rooted in compassion it may be considered unwise to take the example of Anakin Skywalker. To hold him as exemplar of the Jedi is to say very little for the wisdom of that Order. After all, he did grow up to be Darth Vader. However, if we move forward along the Star Wars timeline we see that in *Return of the Jedi*, one of the most respected Jedi, Obi-Wan Kenobi, advocates killing without compassion.

In that movie, just after Master Yoda dies, Obi-Wan advises Luke to destroy Darth Vader. But Luke is hesitant. He believes good still remains in Darth Vader, and he still hopes to help his father turn back to the good side. When he tells the deceased Jedi Knight this, Obi-Wan dismisses Luke's insight, saying Vader's humanity has been "destroyed." He informs Luke that Vader is more a twisted and evil machine than a man. If Obi-Wan's intention truly was Vader's ruin—even if it was for the greater good—it's hard to identify a clear case of compassionate violence here or anywhere else in the Star War series.

For the Jedi to confront violence with compassion they would need to understand first that they are not much different from their opponents. We have seen that life is interconnected. Evil does not exist outside of us. It exists in our own heart. This is the lesson Luke learned in the dark side cave on Dagobah. When we see hatred in another person we cannot truthfully say that hatred exists only in him. If we are honest and we look deeply we will see that person's hatred as a reflection of our own.

The second thing required for the Jedi to compassionately confront violence is that they recognize they are co-responsible for the evil in the world. The dark side does not spring up out of nowhere. All things are a product and a continuation of other phenomena. And all phenomena are bound together in a relationship of interdependence. The Sith, for example, did not appear one day from the sky. They are an offshoot of the Jedi themselves!

According to legend, over a millennia before the events of *The Phantom Menace* a group of Jedi forsook their Order to investigate the Force in a way forbidden by members of the Jedi Council. This group became known as the Dark Lords of the Sith, and they were marked as wholly evil. Shortly after the rise of the Sith, a great war took place where internecine conflict and Jedi intervention brought about the destruction of the Dark Lords. Yet one remained.

He acquired an apprentice, and over the next thousand years the secrets of the Sith were passed from master to apprentice. Century after century the Sith lived in the shadows until the time was ripe for them to reveal themselves and exact their revenge on the Jedi Order. The evil of Darth Maul and the eventual destruction of the Galactic Republic and the Jedi Knights had its beginning in the Jedi Order itself.

If the Jedi were to look deeply it would not be difficult for them to see that this "new" evil came from the heart of "good." The Sith are in fact in the Jedi, and the Jedi are in the Sith. It was Jedi dogma and strictures that stifled some Knights and contributed to their restlessness and subsequent search for greater power. This search came to fruition with the rise of the Empire and the destruction of Alderaan.

Jedi contemporary to the events of *The Phantom Menace* and *Attack of the Clones* also contributed to the rise of evil. Count Dooku, the ringleader of a group of disgruntled star systems and financial conglomerates, was a fallen Jedi. His discontent with the bloated bureaucracy of the Galactic Republic and the failures of the Senate propelled him to seek a new order to replace the decrepit old one. Many Jedi, such as Qui-Gon Jinn, were aware of the corruption in the Senate and could relate to Dooku's yearnings for a better tomorrow. When we look carefully at our enemies we will see ourselves, and we will see how our lives have contributed to their manifestation.

For the Jedi's action to be considered compassionate they must act without anger or hatred, and with the clear understanding that their opponent is not their enemy. When a Jedi sees herself in the Sith she may seek other means of stopping her foe that don't end with a saber across the throat. She will attack only out of necessity to protect others from harm and with compassion for the evildoer.

In *Attack of the Clones*, Mace Windu informs Palpatine that the Jedi are "keepers of the peace, not soldiers." Inside, Palpatine must've been giggling his two-faced head off. For centuries the Sith had been plotting the eradication of the Jedi. Not just the decimation of the Order's numbers, but a complete destruction of their spirit. The Clone Wars were designed to turn the Jedi into exactly what Mace said they weren't—soldiers. The wars would force the Jedi to abandon their values and become killers. By the time Order 66 was executed, the Jedi were already dead.

The issue of the Jedi's failed mission is addressed throughout *The Clone Wars* animated series, particularly in two story arcs: the Lurmen episodes and the Mandlore arc in season two. In that arc the self-described pacifist Duchess Satine calls out Obi-Wan for the Jedi's divergence from their peaceful mandate.

"I remember a time when Jedi were not generals, but peacekeepers," she says.

Obi-Wan is not fazed by her words. He is convinced he is doing what is right to restore peace to the galaxy. "A peacekeeper," he reasons, "belongs on the frontlines of conflict, otherwise he wouldn't be able to do his job."

Buddhists are ideally nonviolent. There couldn't be nonviolence if there weren't people defending pacifists against those who would crush them. Even the great nonviolent victories of the past century—Indian independence and the Civil Rights movement in the United States—were successful because they were able to appeal to authorities whose very power rested in their legal monopoly on violence or because they were able to leverage the economic power of other authorities with that power. Nonviolence and violence are interconnected.

Perhaps the Jedi would not have strayed from their role as peacekeepers if they hadn't allowed their vision to become shrouded by the dark side. Perhaps they would've seen a way to prevent the war and cleanse the corrupt Senate without becoming soldiers. But so much was out of balance even before Qui-Gon had discovered Anakin Skywalker on Tatooine. The Jedi had already become political instruments, proud of their status and arrogant, as Yoda pointed out. War was already upon them when Mace made his declaration about their preferred role. At that point they had no choice but to fight the war to keep the peace. That's the way it always is. Once war is upon us, it's too late to stop it. But that doesn't mean we can't act now to prevent the next conflict. As Duchess Satine argues, "The work of a peacekeeper is to make sure that conflict does not arise." That's no easy task. But it can never be achieved unless we start now. Our actions today create the world of tomorrow.

INDEX

ABOUT THE AUTHOR

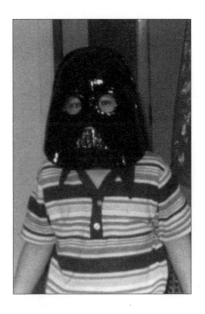

Matthew Bortolin can't remember life without Star Wars. He's been a fan since 1977 and slept on the pavement to see the first screenings of each of the prequel movies. He's handcrafted his own Jedi and Sith robes and built his own lightsaber out of plumbing parts. He became an ordained member of Thich Nhat Hanh's Buddhist community in 2004 and has facilitated meditation groups since. He currently lives in Ventura, California, in the Milky Way Galaxy.

ABOUT WISDOM PUBLICATIONS

Wisdom Publications is the leading publisher of classic and contemporary Buddhist books and practical works on mindfulness. Publishing books from all major Buddhist traditions, Wisdom is a nonprofit charitable organization dedicated to cultivating Buddhist voices the world over, advancing critical scholarship, and preserving and sharing Buddhist literary culture.

To learn more about us or to explore our other books, please visit our website at wisdompubs.org. You can subscribe to our eNewsletter, request a print catalog, and find out how you can help support Wisdom's mission either online or by writing to:

Wisdom Publications
199 Elm Street
Somerville, Massachusetts 02144 USA

You can also contact us at 617-776-7416 or info@wisdom pubs.org.

Wisdom is a 501(c)(3) organization, and donations in support of our mission are tax deductible.

Wisdom Publications is affiliated with the Foundation for the Preservation of the Mahayana Tradition (FPMT).

ALSO AVAILABLE FROM WISDOM PUBLICATIONS

The Dharma of Dragons and Daemons
Buddhist Themes in Modern Fantasy
David R. Loy and Linda Goodhew
Foreword by Jane Hirshfield

"Eloquent. Loy and Goodhew find Buddhist truths in contempary non-Buddhist stories. Pullman's dead are released to become images of interpermeation reminiscient of Thich Nhat Hanh's teachings. Frodo's quest is not to find a treasure or slay a dragon, but to let go. Thus, aspects of Buddhist teachings come alive for children of the West." `
—*Inquiring Mind*

Hardcore Zen
Punk Rock, Monster Movies, and the Truth about Reality
Brad Warner

"Entertaining, bold, and refreshingly direct, this book is likely to change the way one experiences other books about Zen—and maybe even the way one experiences reality."
—*Publishers Weekly* [starred review]

Saltwater Buddha

A Surfer's Quest to Find Zen on the Sea

Jaimal Yogis

"Heartfelt, honest, and deceptively simple. It's great stuff with the words 'Cult Classic' stamped all over it."
—Alex Wade, author of *Surf Nation*

You Are Not Here

And Other Works of Buddhist Fiction

Edited by Keith Kachtick

Foreword by Lama Surya Das

"Drawing on the ancient appeal of 'Tell me a story,' Keith Kachtick has brought together a volume of exquisite tales that breathe with the living spirit of the Dharma."
—Lin Jensen, author of *Bad Dog!*

Money, Sex, War, Karma

Notes for a Buddhist Revolution

David R. Loy

"A flashy title, but a serious and substantial book."
—*Buddhadharma*

The World Is Made of Stories
David R. Loy

"Loy's book is like the self: layer after layer peels away, and the center is empty. But the pleasure is exactly in the exploration. At once Loy's most accessible and most philosophical work."—Alan Senauke for *Buddhadharma*

Buddhism for Dudes
A Jarhead's Field Guide to Mindfulness
Gerry Stribling

"*Buddhism for Dudes* shoots straight and doesn't blink. It's John Wayne meets Zen, complete with all the wisdom and tough-guy charm you'd expect."
—Matthew Bortolin, author of *The Dharma of Star Wars*